Pickups for Hiccups

Pickups for Hiccups

Big Solutions for **Small** Problems

Simon and Hazel Robinson

AMBASSADOR INTERNATIONAL
Greenville, South Carolina • Belfast, Northern Ireland

PICKUPS FOR HICCUPS
Big Solutions for Small Problems

ISBN 978-1-84030-194-6

Ambassador Publications
a division of
Ambassador Productions Ltd.
Providence House
Ardenlee Street,
Belfast,
BT6 8QJ
Northern Ireland
www.ambassador-productions.com

Emerald House
427 Wade Hampton Blvd.
Greenville
SC 29609, USA

Dedicated to our mothers
Jo Robinson and Yvonne Thorn

Contents

Introduction
Hiccups are no joke!

IT BEGINS as a small shudder at the back of the throat and within a few moments it grows into a shrill squeak that will amuse everyone except you. Every few words you speak become punctuated by a judder and the more you try to stop it the stronger it seems to become. While hiccups are not disastrous they can be exasperating.

You will undoubtedly have had this experience. Of course it does not last forever: after a while the squeaks grow quieter and weaker until they finally die away. Hiccups are not life threatening or dangerous but for a time they can be very disruptive.

Small can be serious

There have been many good books written about coping with difficulties and trials but few deal with the little problems which — while they will not overwhelm you — can disrupt your life for a period of time. For example: you have a great quiet time which has focussed you on living for the Lord throughout the coming day. You close your Bible, put on your coat and sprint out of the door with a 'hallelujah' and a 'praise the Lord' on your lips. When you put your key in the ignition your car splutters out a few sounds of protest that seem to be telling you that it has no intention of moving. The rescue company are so busy that they will not be able to get there for at least an hour and you are going to miss the most important meeting of the week. Suddenly your sense of purpose can evaporate and your mood can change from one of expectation to frustration.

This could never be considered to be a big trial and within a couple of hours it will be sorted out; tomorrow you may even be laughing about it but today it seems to have stifled the blessing you had in your quiet time and the sense of purpose you began the day with.

It has been a great Sunday service; the preaching has spoken to you, the music has been outstanding and you have been conscious of God's presence. When it finishes you stroll over to the crèche area to collect your child and you are looking forward to seeing her again. You can see her through the window and give a little wave but she does not seem very happy. Then you look round and see another parent – who happened to be the 'drama queen' of the church - shooting angry looks in your direction. 'Your daughter has just assaulted mine in the crèche', she growls, 'what are you going to do about it?' You try and reason with her but she is determined to turn a little skirmish into a major battle.

When your car pulls into the drive you are no longer humming the song that was going through your mind at the end of the service, instead you are replaying the angry conflict in your head. One encounter outside the crèche seems to have wiped out the blessing you had been enjoying that morning.

When James says that we 'face trials of many kinds' he uses a word describing big and small difficulties. The problems that have just been described may seem minor but they are not harmless and they can inflict damage on one's spiritual life if not handled properly. That is why we need pickups for these hiccups.

In this book we will look at small, but significant, problems encountered at home, church, the workplace, school and college and identify Biblical and practical solutions that will equip us to rise above them.

Chapter One

Hiccups at home

MONEY'S TOO TIGHT TO MENTION

There is nothing quite like a night out with good friends especially when you have not seen each other for a long time. It is great to catch up with their news: what is happening in their family, how their jobs are going and what kind of Christian service they are involved in. A lot of our friends have excelled in their careers and we are pleased to hear about the way they have been able to climb the corporate ladder with their ethics intact and their witness clear. However there is one problem with evenings like this: being a pastor Simon is not paid a huge salary (and that is not a complaint) so we have to scour the menu for the least expensive dishes while our friends can choose what they like without worrying about the cost. There was a time, during the early years of Simon's ministry, when we took our children on a Church outing and could not even afford to buy them ice creams. Looking back at those times we rejoice in the way God provided for our needs but we also remember that life can be tough when money is 'too tight to mention'.

If you have been in this situation you will know how difficult it is when your children come home from school asking for the latest designer trainers

– which all of their friends are wearing – while you can only afford to buy them a cheap imitation. Or when your friends are going on holiday to a luxury resort in an exotic location when all you can manage is a few days in a caravan in England. Although you tell yourself that money is not everything and that you have a lot to be thankful for, you will feel it deep down inside.

Dangerous territory

There is something about water that draws children. No doubt you have happy memories of playing in a river or lake as a child but the likelihood is that your parents were the ones who made you aware of the notice saying 'danger – deep water'. What appeared to be harmless could have been lethal if you had ignored the dangers lying beneath the surface. The same can be said for this problem and you need to be aware of the hidden threats that will cause spiritual harm if they are ignored.

The most obvious is that 'green-eyed monster' - jealousy. You can smile sweetly, and nod with apparent interest when your friend enthuses about their brand new car but you are painfully aware of something gnawing inside you. And this is often accompanied by a little voice in your head saying 'why should she get all the nice things? It is just not fair!' If left unchecked it will continue, affecting your attitude, poisoning your heart and leaving a distance between you and God. You may also become discontent with your life and ungrateful for the things God has given you. The simple, spiritual aims that you once had become buried by ambitions for wealth, prosperity and material possessions and your focus shifts away from God's Kingdom to the things this world offers.

At this stage the possibility of credit cards and loans may enter into your thinking as way of being able to buy the things you could not normally afford. The companies offering them seldom stress the fact that at the end of the day you will still have to come up with the money, plus a considerable amount of interest. Sadly some Christians have fallen into this trap and have ended up being saddled with huge debts which cast a shadow over their lives.

Remember, remember

The likely root of the difficulties will lay in wrong perceptions that need to be challenged by the truth. Here are three facts that should be embedded in your mind at all times.

Fact one: You have a priceless tag

The society we live in is obsessed with wealth and glamour. There does not seem to be a day that passes without a TV programme or a newspaper giving an account of a lavish party that a celebrity has thrown or details of their fortune. A British newspaper reported that the wealth of Britain's richest 1,000 stood at almost 99 billion pounds in April 2007. Our culture is fascinated with wealth and gives status to those who have the largest fortunes. The Bible however, gives us a radically different perspective: we are told that, 'The brother in humble circumstances ought to take pride in his high position. But the one who is rich should take pride in his low position, because he will pass away like a wild flower' (James 1:9-10). God does not look at you in terms of how much money you have but in terms of the price his Son has paid to make you part of his family (see Acts 20:28).

Fact two: You have a Heavenly Father

In the early years of ministry we did not always know how we were going to meet the next bill that came in the post. During that time we often clung onto a verse that said: 'I was young and now I am old, yet I have never seen the righteous forsaken or their children begging bread' (Psalm 37:25). And our experience proved it to be true: our Heavenly Father provided for all our needs. We can remember many wonderful ways in which the right amount of money turned up through a gift in the post, in a repayment that we were not expecting or a supermarket's special offer that helped us to afford something we required.

Jesus picked one of the beautiful flowers that grew in Galilee as he spoke to the crowd gathered on the mountain. It was delicate, intricate and would have been admired by anyone who would take the time to look at it. 'Do you see this flower?' He said, 'not even Solomon in all his splendour was dressed like one of these.' People in the crowd would have nodded and realised that they had never quite appreciated them in that way before. Jesus reminded them how quickly these beautiful little objects of creation passed away saying: 'If that is how God clothes the grass of the field, which is here today and tomorrow is thrown into the fire will he not much more clothe you, O you of little faith' (Matt 6:29-30). It stands to reason that if God has saved us through the death and resurrection of his Son, brought us into his family and secured our future in heaven he will provide for our needs in this life.

Fact three: You are a citizen of heaven

One of the most difficult things about a long flight is joining the immigration line on arrival. You have just spent hours in a metal tube being hurtled through the sky at hundreds of miles an hour and you are tired and disorientated. However you must complete forms and answer questions before you are allowed to enter the country. Going through immigration is a stark reminder that the place you are visiting is not where you really belong. It is a relief to finish a trip and walk through the exit for citizens of your own country.

In the New Testament, Christians are described as 'citizens of heaven' (Phil 3:20). This world offers many pleasures and rewards; some of them are completely legitimate while others are not but we must always remember that we do not belong to it. God has much better things in store for us and to focus our ambition on possessions and wealth is a betrayal of our true citizenship.

Relating to the rich

How do you handle the difference in lifestyle between you and your friend who enjoys exotic holidays, lives in a huge house and drives a brand new car?

• Acceptance

Amy Carmichael penned some insightful words during her life but some of the most profound were 'in acceptance lies peace'. Instead of wondering why you are not as wealthy as your friend, accept the position God has put you in, remembering that from a heavenly perspective you have the higher place (James 1:9-10). Of course that does not mean that you should never seek promotion or embrace circumstances that offer you a more comfortable income but if there is nothing you can do to change your circumstances accept them as the Lord's will for you and get on with living for him.

• Contentment

What kind of image comes into your mind at the mention of contentment? For many it would be sitting on a golden sandy beach and listening to the waves gently lap against the shore whilst sipping an ice cold drink. However in the New Testament it is linked to someone who was in prison because of his faith in Christ! The Apostle Paul was waiting for news of an appeal he had made to the Emperor. During this time he wrote to the Church at Philippi to thank them for the gift they had sent him. Since he had been teaching them some important truths, Paul wanted to be sure they realised that he was able to be content in any circumstances, so he spoke about his situation. 'I know what it is to be in need,' he wrote 'And I know what it is to have plenty. I have learned the secret of being content whatever the circumstances' (Phil 4:12). The word that Paul used describes 'self sufficiency' or 'satisfaction' in the sense that he was not dependent upon anything or anyone other than the Lord. Thank God for the times of prosperity but keep trusting him when your circumstances change, knowing that when God is all you have he is all you need. This is the key to contentment and if you squander your time and energy chasing a better lifestyle you will never be satisfied because there will always be more to pursue. After warning Timothy of the dangers of craving to be rich Paul said:

' . . . godliness with contentment is great gain. For we brought nothing into the world, and we can take nothing out of it. But if we have food and clothing, we will be content with that' (1 Tim 6:6-7).

• Appreciate your friend

Society today assesses people in terms of how much money they earn and what they possess but as Christians we have a very different view of people. Jesus said 'Watch out! Be on your guard against all kinds of greed; a man's life does not consist in the abundance of his possessions'(Luke 12:15). When you have friends who have been blessed with wealth treat them as you would anyone else and appreciate them for who they are and not what they earn or their position in society.

DEALING WITH MONEY PROBLEMS

Having been made aware of these dangers and encouraged by the facts have been identified, you will be in a strong position to tackle money problems. Here are some practical steps that you can now take.

Step one: Budget

In the lean financial times we faced it would have been all too easy to bury our heads in the sand and carry on spending money. However we decided to take a deep breath and face up to the challenge by working out our costs and setting a budget for each month. We began with the most significant payments such as the mortgage, council tax, electricity and heating and then we allocated what remained for food and clothes. We cannot look back on those times and tell you that budgeting was fun but it did help us evaluate what we were facing. If our expenditure had outstripped income, Simon was prepared to take some casual work to make up the difference but thankfully that was never necessary and he was able to give his whole time to ministry.

One thing that will make budgeting more bearable is to set a little money aside for treats – even when times are hard you will need them!

Step two: Buy from Charity shops

When our finances were tight some of our best clothes came from charity shops. Our children were dressed in designer gear that we could never have afforded in the high street shops and Hazel was often graced with elegant dresses. True, at first it took a good dose of humility to start rummaging through the clothes in such shops but it provided us with a life-line. Also we never refused offers of clothes which our friend's children had outgrown. E Bay or the local papers are a great resource for finding second-hand baby equipment and toys. Contrary to popular opinion young children do not mind playing with second hand toys or wearing clothes that have been passed on.

Step three: Plan ahead

Hazel is a true 'Proverbs 31' woman. During the years when we had a monthly battle with the bank balance she was on the constant look out for special offers and reductions. If a toy was being sold off just after Christmas or in the middle of the year she would buy it and store it away so that when the a birthday or Christmas came we were not squeezed for cash. And if food or commodities were reduced she would buy extra so that we could save money for the weeks and months ahead.

Step four: Get advice

Never be afraid to ask advice or get help. If you have lost your job and cannot make the mortgage payments speak to the mortgage company immediately so that arrangements can be made. Older people will probably have been through similar problems and their advice will be invaluable. Naturally the first channels for advice should be from Christian sources. We recommend Rob Parson's 'The Money Secret Book' but there are also some excellent secular resources providing helpful and sensible advice. Martin Lewis' website moneysavingexpert.com is full of practical advice about budgeting and how to make your money stretch further.

Step five: Pray

After reading the earlier part of the chapter you should have a solid fact embedded in your mind: your Heavenly Father cares for all of your needs (see Matt 6:25-34). Never think that your money problems are too small or trivial to bring to God: he cares about them and will hear your prayer and provide for you. And pray with an open Bible in front of you so that you can make your requests to God in line with the promises he has made. Thousands of years ago a man named Nehemiah who was a long way from his own country heard some distressing news from home and cried out to God in prayer. As he did so he cited a promise God had made through Solomon, that if the people returned to God he would 'gather them … and bring them to the place [he] had chosen as a dwelling for [his] name' (Neh 1:9). The Puritan Matthew Henry comments on Nehemiah's prayer by saying that 'our best pleas and prayers come from the promises of God .'[1] If you are unsure of which passages to turn to here are some suggestions:

'Honor the Lord with your wealth,
with the firstfruits of all your crops;
then your barns will be filled to overflowing,
and your vats will brim over with new wine.
(Proverbs 3:9-10)

'For the Lord God is a sun and shield;
the Lord bestows favour and honour;
no good thing does he withhold
from those whose walk is blameless.'
(Psalm 84:11)

---

1. Henry, M. (1996, c1991). Matthew Henry's commentary on the whole Bible : Complete and unabridged in one volume (Ne 1:5). Peabody: Hendrickson.

'Do not be like them, for your Father knows what you need before you ask him.
"This, then, is how you should pray:
" 'Our Father in heaven . . .'
(Matthew 6:8-9)

'If you, then, though you are evil, know how to give good gifts to your children, how much more will your Father in heaven give good gifts to those who ask him!'
(Matthew 7:11)

'And my God will meet all your needs according to his glorious riches in Christ Jesus.'
(Philippians 4:19)

'As it is written:
"He has scattered abroad his gifts to the poor;
his righteousness endures for ever."[a]
'Now he who supplies seed to the sower and bread for food will also supply and increase your store of seed and will enlarge the harvest of your righteousness.'
(2 Corinthians 9:9-10)

Step six: Tithe

When money is in short supply there is a danger that the first expense you cut back on will be your giving to God's work. However God's Word commands us to give a proportion of our income to him in a cheerful and sacrificial way (see 1 Cor 9:13-14)

Simon's grandmother had a wise saying: 'money is a good servant but a terrible master.' That is true whether you are wealthy or hard-up. If you have a lot of money your life can be centred on material things rather than on the Lord and if you have little you can spend all of your time worrying about your

---

a. Psalm 112:9.

finances or trying to work out ways to improve them. Do everything you can to make sure that financial hiccups do not dominate your life.

KIDS AT WAR

If we could choose what family life would be like we would all opt for the soft-tinted images on TV adverts depicting happy parents holding hands with perfect-looking children doing everything their parents say without question or protest. It was not long after we became parents that we discovered reality was very different! It is both a delight and a privilege to be parents but broken nights, lost sleep, dirty nappies and sibling rivalry come with the territory. Not to mention the heartache of having your child come home in tears because he or she has been bullied at school or when a fight breaks out between your children and your best friend's kids.

Hiccups like these can have a significant effect on your spiritual life. You can succumb to anger at your own children or at someone else's and frustration that you can never get anything done because you seem to be constantly breaking up fights. Then there are times when you see another parent handle their children with seemingly impressive parenting skills and you feel totally inadequate. What are the pickups for these hiccups?

Realism

We have all known families who give the impression that they are as near to perfect as possible but behind closed doors they can be quite different. We visited a church where the wives wore flowery long dresses and pretty hats, their boys wore cute little suits with bow-ties while the girls were dressed like little princesses. The teenagers shunned rock music and never talked back to their parents. But when we dug below the surface we found that it was all a façade: the teenagers had learned to fit the image their parents had shaped for them but did some very different things when their backs were turned. And in private the children threw tantrums and had days when they were cranky.

One of the biggest problems we may have is a sense of guilt and inadequacy because we wrongly assume that no-one else has the same parenting struggles we face, but a healthy sense of realism will soon knock that away.

Children are sinners

When David made his heartfelt confession of sin in Psalm 51, he said, 'surely I have been a sinner from birth, sinful from the time my mother conceived me' (Psalm 51:5). Every child – with the exception of Jesus – was born as a sinner. So we should not be surprised that our children show sinful tendencies. Of course that does not excuse sin but it does explain why our children scream at us, hit-out, throw their food on the floor and fight with other children: they were born that way.

Children need correction

Simon will never forget the time when he first went bowling; he swapped his trainers for a smelly pair of lightweight shoes provided by the bowling alley, picked up the heaviest ball he could lay his hands on and threw it at the skittles imagining that it would follow a straight line. To his surprise it quickly veered off course and disappeared down the gully. He discovered that bowling was a much more skilled practice than he first imagined because the ball had a bias which he had to compensate for.

When someone argues with Simon about the Bible's teaching that every person is born a sinner (which we often call 'original sin') he asks them whether you need to teach a child to do wrong. The answer of course is 'no'; we teach a child to do what is right but wrong seems to come quite naturally. That is why the Bible tells us to 'Train a child in the way he should go, and when he is old he will not turn from it' (Prov 22.6). There may be times when your children delight and surprise you with good and thoughtful acts but they will also sin and you need to correct them and teach them to pursue what is right. The book of Proverbs, which is packed full of priceless wisdom, is set in the context of a father teaching his son and reminding him of the things his mother has taught him.

'Listen, my son, to your father's instruction and do not forsake your mother's teaching. They will be a garland to grace your head and a chain to adorn your neck.' (Proverbs 1:8-9).

Children are erratic

Our hearts always go out to a parent standing over a screaming child who has thrown herself on the floor of the supermarket. We feel like putting a hand on their shoulder and saying 'we know how you feel because we have been there too!' One minute your child can be happily following the shopping trolley and suddenly they see something they want and throw a tantrum when you tell them that they cannot have it. Adults usually behave in a logical way but children are erratic: they will want to do the very thing that is not possible, eat something at the most unsuitable time or go somewhere that is out of bounds. And no amount of reasoning will get through to them.

Parents have blind spots

You can say all sorts of things about your children's behaviour to your husband or wife but if another person accuses them of misbehaving you will find your protective instinct quickly kicking in. If your child gets involved in a fight you will assume it is the other child's fault or if someone says that your child has lied or stolen you will undoubtedly respond with horror and say 'my Darren would never do that.' Be aware of those blind-spots and listen carefully to what the person has to say before you respond to them.

WAR ON THE HOME FRONT

It is Monday morning, you have a pile of ironing to catch up on so you get the toys out and hope that your children will play quietly. It works – for a little while – until you hear a yelp, then the sound of Lego being thrown across the room and little screeches piercing the air; once again civil war has disrupted the peace. Most of us – on more than one occasion – have charged in and shouted at our children, which might temporarily relieve our own frustration but in the long it will do no good. We would not want to give the impression that we have been perfect parents. We have taken that route on many occasions but we have learned from our mistakes and would like to share the lessons with you.

Take a deep breath

The old saying goes: 'fools rush in where angels fear to tread.' It would be helpful to remember this before marching in to stop the sibling skirmish. James urges us to 'be slow to speak and slow to become angry' (James 1:19) which will be a very useful principle to apply to this situation. Sure, they will make a lot of noise, push each other and throw a few things around the room but it would be much better to stop for a minute, take a deep breath and ask God to give you the strength and wisdom to handle this in a way that honours him. Hold on to the promise: 'if any of you lacks wisdom let him ask of God who gives generously to all without finding fault' (James 1:5). This little fight may seem trivial in the light of all the other troubles going on in the world but it matters to you and more importantly it matters to God. The verse assures us that he will not criticise our parenting skills but give us the light we need to understand what is going on and use it as a positive lesson for our children.

Divide and rule!

If you stand between the warring factions demanding to know what has happened, the argument will continue - with you as the channel. The most effective thing to do is to separate them and find something that will distract. When tempers simmer down you can try to find out what has happened but for the time being your primary mission is to establish a ceasefire.

Teach them

When things are finally quiet say a few words about how important it is to share things and to be kind to each other. Tell them about Jesus and the example he has set for them. Ask them how they think how he would have treated his brothers and sisters when he was growing up in Mary and Joseph's family.

Encourage them

While it is important to tell children when their behaviour is unacceptable it is also very healthy to encourage them when they are doing the right thing. Simon and his sister fought like cat and dog and there were times when they drove their mother to distraction (which she still likes to remind him about!). Sometimes their grandma looked after them for an afternoon and when they played quietly and got on well with each other she would tell them how nice it was and say 'wouldn't it be lovely if you could do that for your mum.' Those words went a long way to improve their behaviour.

Get a sense of perspective

When one of these skirmishes breaks out you may be inclined to tell them that they are always fighting but you will know this is not really accurate. These problems can seem much bigger if you get them out of perspective and talk about them as if they happen 24/7. Tell yourself that this is what children sometimes do and be thankful that it is not all of the time. You could even thank God for the good days he has given you when the children have got along well.

Sibling rivalry

We found it a challenge and a joy to make all the necessary adjustments when our first child was born. The greatest benefit was that we could devote time to one child but when number two came along it was not quite so easy.

There will inevitably be times when the oldest child is not best pleased that they do not get the attention they once enjoyed. This can be a drain on parents and there is a danger of over-reacting to something the eldest child is doing in order to get attention. So it is important to have some basic principles to smooth the way.

Accept it

There have been times when every parent has asked 'why is he so jealous of his new sister?' However this is a natural reaction to a big change in their circumstances and in time it will run its course. Just accept that it is normal.

Involve them

It can be very effective to involve the other children in something you are doing for the new baby even if they may prolong what you are doing. A small task like asking them to bring some cotton wool over may not seem particularly significant to you but it will mean a lot to your child. He or she will feel part of their new brother or sister's life.

Make time for them

One of the most difficult issues for the eldest child is that you are not able to give them the same amount of time as you used to be able to. Do whatever you can to make some time – no matter how short it may seem to you – when the two of you can be together. It may be just sitting down to watch a TV programme or reading a story to them, but it is a special period when the two of you are together.

BULLYING

Simon's mum's anxiety levels were already high. He was half an hour late home and she was anxiously waiting at the door for him. When he staggered over the doormat and slumped onto the sofa with a black eye and torn shirt she was demanding some answers. Her questions came thick and fast: 'Where have you been?', 'What has happened to you?', 'Why have you got a black eye – has someone been hitting you?' Repositioning himself he tried to talk his way out of it: 'It's nothing mum, I just fell over and tore my shirt. That's why I'm a bit late.' Of course she did not believe a word and refused to move until he told her the whole story. Simon could not say why he did not want her to know that he had been set upon by some other boys; it may have been pride or even a sense of independency but it took a lot of persuading to get the information out of him. We had the same problem on the occasions when we had suspicions that our children had been bullied, but taking a leaf from Simon's mother's book we were determined to get to the bottom of it and do something to help them.

Bullying comes in all shapes and sizes – from cruel taunting to physical beatings – but it should be taken seriously and will always be a source of distress to parents. If it has intruded into one of your children's lives you may have instinctively wanted to march up to the school and deal some swift justice to the children concerned, probably causing greater problems.

Pray

This is one of the 'trials of many kinds' described by James (James 1:2) and as such is an opportunity for your faith to grow and for you to show your child how to face problems as a Christian. Pray with them and continue to bring it to your Heavenly Father in your own prayer times.

Handle your own anger

When you find out what has happened to your child you will be dealing with two powerful emotions: deep concern and anger at the way he or she has been treated. Both are totally legitimate responses but anger has the potential to grow into something that will poison your heart and affect your relationship with God. That is why James warns that 'man's anger does not bring about the righteous life that God desires' (James 1:20). Also in Ephesians we are told: 'Do not let the sun go down while you are still angry and do not give the devil a foothold' (Eph 4:26-27). Make sure that you have your anger prayerfully under control and that your main concern is for your child's well being.

Re-assure your child

Many parents have responded to the news that their child has been bullied by declaring that they will go up to the school the next day to get the children responsible punished. However it would be better to begin by re-assuring your child that everything will be all right. At times like this they are not interested in bullies getting into trouble but in being comforted and put at ease.

Get the facts

After giving your child a little time, get the facts from him or her and discreetly make a note of them so that you have something solid to bring to the school when you make your visit.

Deal with it

If the bullying occurs at school go and visit the teacher. This is an opportunity to 'let your light shine' if you deal with it in a way that will glorify the Lord. Be polite and fair but be firm. Continue to monitor the situation by regular contact with the school and be prepared to take further action if they do not take it seriously. You may need to take specialist advice. There are some helpful websites and resources available such as: **childline.org.uk**; **www.careforthefamily.org.uk**; **anti-bullyingalliance.org.uk**, and **www.beatbullying.org**.

The power of a good witness

A teenager badly beat up another boy at his school. The next day he was summoned to the Head Teacher's office because the father of the boy he had attacked wanted to meet him. At the time he thought that this was going to be a very uncomfortable experience but when the man concerned was ushered through the door he went straight up to him, shook his hand and said, 'Hello son, we have a few things to sort out.' The man was a Christian and he dealt with the matter in such a positive and forgiving way that it impressed the young man. A few months later he became a Christian, seeing this encounter as a significant part of the process of challenging him.

Family life never quite fits the idealistic images you see on adverts, films and even on the cover of Christian magazines! There will be times when it seems as if war has broken out under your roof. Although this can be very difficult it is also an opportunity to see God do great things in your family and for you to grow in your relationship with him.

A NEW BABY IN THE HOUSE

A few days after our first child was born the Pastor's wife rang up to see how we were getting on. She had a wonderful way of putting across hard truths gently. Our son was due to arrive at Christmas and we were very pleased that he came a week early. 'At least we can have a normal Christmas now he has been born,' Simon said. And in her own sweet way she brought us back to reality: 'Dear boy,' she replied with a chuckle, 'when you have a baby in the house life will never be normal'. In the days, weeks and months that followed we discovered this for ourselves. A new baby will turn life upside down. Simon soon learned this when he settled down to watch his favourite TV programme only to find it punctuated by crying and nappy changes.

Naturally it is a joy to have a new baby in the house but the new arrival will bring its own little problems.

Loss of routine

When a new baby comes into the house routine goes out of the window. Not only is this disorientating, it may also have a spiritual effect because it becomes difficult to set aside time to spend with God and to read his Word. And you will rarely be able to attend home groups or midweek meetings together.

Deprived of basics

Babies are so demanding that for a little while you will not even be able to take a shower, eat meals or even dress when you want to. The home seems to be under the baby's rule and do not be surprised if tidiness seems to be a thing of the past!

Someone's come between us

It is quite ironic that someone who started out from an act of intimacy can stifle it once he or she arrives! Simon wonders whether babies have a special sense that made them cry as soon as their parents have a cuddle. But for a time the simplest acts of affection can be constantly interrupted.

Broken nights

When we first became parents the days when we were able to put our head on the pillow in the blissful assumption that we would not wake until the next morning seemed as if they belonged to a different life. Nights were disturbed by feeds and bouts of crying so that solid sleep was a thing of the past. This could also make the following day difficult to cope with.

Survival Guide

We have the benefit of looking back on these problems with two decades' distance. The good news is that these times will pass but the reality is that they can be tough and seem never-ending when you are going through them. Here is a basic survival guide we have put together.

Remember that God understands

You may have expected to be 'super-mum' or 'super-dad': able to keep up with your church commitments, read huge chunks of the Bible and spend hours in prayer whilst changing nappies and fitting in feeds. But this was never God's expectation. The Bible tells us that 'he knows how we are formed, he remembers that we are dust' (Psalm 103:14). He knows everything about you, even the number of hairs on your head (Matt 10:30) – although you may have pulled a few out since the new baby arrived! God knows 'when [you] sit and when [you] rise' and he 'perceives your thoughts from afar' (Psalm 139:2). In addition to all this 'he gently leads those that have young' (Isaiah 40:11). God has never loved you because you read the Bible and pray for hours every day; he loves you because he loves you and for no other reason!

God is among the pots and pans

The Spanish mystic Teresa of Ávila reminded her readers that 'God lives also among the pots and pans.' In other words, he is not just with you when you are in prayer but when you are going about the business of life; no matter how mundane that may seem. Most of the jobs you have to do when a new baby arrives seem a world away from your quiet time but all of these things are about establishing a new life in this world and this is something you can do to the glory of God, conscious that you are in his presence.

Grab and pray!

If you are a young mum it will be rare to get a moment to yourself but when this does happen try your best to give priority to reading a few verses from God's Word. You need to be realistic and read short segments but it will keep the communication channels with God open. Dads may be able to grab a bit of time during lunch or stop off for a moment when they are on the road. Try to be realistic but consistent. This is not easy but it is possible.

Get together

Christian mums often form Bible Study and prayer groups so find out if there is one near you and get involved in it. Hazel has been in many such groups as we have moved around the country and has always found them an invaluable source of support. If there are none in your neighbourhood find some Christian mums and start one yourself. You do not have to have deep studies just share a bit of time in God's Word together and pray for one another. Some of Hazel's most treasured times have been invested in groups like this.

Reach out to mums who are not Christians too by getting to know them in local parent and toddler groups. Having children of the same age creates an instant bond and will give you great opportunities for friendship evangelism.

Bring in the babysitters

It may be a little while before you are able or prepared to leave your baby in someone else's care. However it is extremely important to get some time when you can concentrate on each other without worrying about the children. Perhaps the grandparents could look after them for an hour or two. When they are older you could arrange with friends to have each others children for an afternoon.

THE TROUBLE WITH TODDLERS

Being grandparents is great! In fact Simon says he thinks it is so good he wishes he had done it first! As we write this book our little grandson has started walking and has clearly made the transition from baby to toddler. We asked our daughter-in-law to tell us about some of the challenges this has brought to their home-life and we could hardly keep up with her so this is completely up-to-date.

Tantrums

You can see it coming from a mile off: it starts with a little tear, develops into a red face and then erupts in an ear piercing scream usually timed to cause the parent the most embarrassment possible. Unfortunately if you have a toddler, tantrums are a painful fact of life. Here are a few points to help you navigate this difficult and emotive territory.

Call out to God

Nehemiah does not say anything about bringing up toddlers but he does set an example we can apply to toddler tantrums.

He was the cupbearer to the King of Persia and was expected to look serene all the time he was in active service. One day he had received some distressing news from home and the King asked him why he looked so sad. Nehemiah tells us that at this point he was 'very much afraid'. After explaining the reason for his sad expression the King asked him what he wanted and Nehemiah says that he 'prayed to the God of heaven' before he gave an answer (see Nehemiah 2:1-5). That would not have been a protracted time of prayer behind closed doors but a quick, quiet cry for help; which the Lord answered.

Throughout this book we have emphasised the fact that God cares about the little problems in your life so do not hesitate to call out a quick two-word prayer: 'help Lord.'

Don't give in

When you are tired and your child is screaming the house down because he or she cannot have something they want you may be tempted to give in for a quiet life. We have done it on more than one occasion and can tell you that although it will give a little respite, in the long term it will only make things worse.

Distraction: the parent's powerful weapon

While a tantrum can flare up very quickly it can disappear almost as fast. The key is to distract your child so that they become occupied with something else; try being proactive by having some things ready when it happens. You can play a familiar game with them or draw their attention to something that will occupy their interest. We should add one word of caution: do not make this seem as if you are rewarding bad behaviour with a treat.

All bad things come to an end

You would have to be crazy to enjoy the sound of a child wailing; it is like a siren and your instinctive reaction will be to do anything you can to stop it. If all the above has failed relax in the knowledge that it will not last forever, sooner or later your child will run out of steam and get too tired to carry on. There is no point in becoming so stressed that you get exhausted— then you will not get the benefit of the quietness that follows.

'The wants'

Simon's grandma had a wonderful way of using humour with children to defuse tense situations. When our children were demanding sweets and toys we followed her example. One of us would say 'oh dear you are not well again – you've got the wants!' It always ended the demands and after we had all laughed about it we had to explain that we could not afford to give them everything they asked for. However, this made the presents we were able to give them all the more special.

More little troubles

There are so many challenges bound up with these little packages of life that the list is endless. They like to feed themselves but rarely hit their mouth on the first attempt and take great delight in throwing food on the floor. Once they are mobile, they will be eager to explore their environment and they will gravitate to the most dangerous and unsuitable places. Cupboards will get emptied, ornaments knocked onto the floor, TV controls will be taken on a tour of the house and DVD players will be tested on their capacity to consume cake. This is also a very artistic time in their development so watch out for your newly decorated wall: it will make a great canvas for their latest work of art. What you need most of all to handle this is a good sense of humour. You can do your best and try to prevent all these things but be assured some will slip through the net and it is all part of growing up. When Simon was at Theological College an African Christian used to tell him not to worry when the children got up to mischief: 'if my children sat quietly all day I'd get very worried and would end up with a big doctor's bill' he would say. Of course bad behaviour must be discouraged and when necessary punished but this is a time when toddlers are making their first clumsy attempts to explore the world around them so cut them some slack: let children be children and thank God for them.

HELP – THERE'S A TEENAGER IN MY HOUSE!

If your children are teenagers you wonder how your delightful little boy or girl has turned into the person sprawled across the couch in your lounge. Let us encourage you: we struggled too and reached the other end of it with a better relationship with our sons than we had before. If you have turned to this part of the book in the hope that it will help to resolve all of your problems with teenagers we should remind you that this is about small problems. However if you want to deal with those little issues to smooth the path of those difficult years read on.

Independence issues

There was a day when your child loved to go wherever you went and hold your hand at every possible opportunity but when the teenage years arrive that will belong to the dim and distant past. The natural thing is to take this personally but we can assure you that it is just their way of asserting their independence. This is the time when they begin to break free from the family (in the best sense) and begin to strike out on their own; other cultures have ushered young people into adulthood at this stage.

Distance

The most painful part of this phase is the distance it can create between you and your child. Your questions will often be met by one word answers and your suggestions with derisive grunts. You will have to work very hard to get any information from them and be very careful of what you say about their friends. At times it will seem as if there is a huge gulf between you.

Arguments

The little person who used to respond instantly to a telling off has been replaced by someone who will be prepared to argue with you about anything. Do not expect to win: they will always have an answer and will be convinced that they are right. Although this can be quite annoying to you it is another important aspect of their development; they are testing out their perspective on life and the world around them and you are the ideal person to practice on! Naturally you must insist on respect but always listen to their arguments; they may even be right on some occasions.

'What do you know anyway?'

Mark Twain has been quoted as saying 'When I was a boy of fourteen, my father was so ignorant I could hardly stand to have the old man around. But when I got to be twenty-one, I was astonished at how much the old man had learned in seven years.' That saying accurately sums up the disdain teenagers often have towards their parents. Be prepared to have your opinions shredded, your taste in music dismissed and your dress sense scoffed at; it is all part of having a teenager in the house.

Music, sleep and noise

Teenage behaviour is full of irony. When they are little it can be difficult to get them to sleep and they rarely allow you a lie in but as soon they hit the teenage years they seem to be covered in a shroud of sleep until lunch-time. Although you may not be able to get a lot of conversation from them there is often loud music – the kind the neighbours do not particularly enjoy – blaring from their stereos. At times like this parents ought to put a notice on their door saying 'beware - teenager in the house'.

Staring at the screen

One of the most common problems with teenagers in this technology-driven generation is that they will spend hours staring at a computer screen or sending text messages to their friends. Communication is only cool if it comes through some kind of electronic device.

You have to accept this is a contemporary mind-set but it is important to be on the look out for signs that they may be getting drawn into the dark realms of the web. Here are some important questions to ask:

- Do they hide their Internet searches from the rest of the family?
- Do they spend a lot of time on the net after everyone has gone to bed?
- Do they object more angrily than usual when you ask them to log off?
- Have they become more distant than you may have expected?

The inclination you will have as a parent is to rush in and demand to see what they are looking at. The likely result is that they will put their defences up, angrily deny that they have been looking at anything unhealthy and accuse you of trying to control them. Try a gentle approach; perhaps even telling them that every time you log on you are aware of the dangers posed to yourself. If they have been browsing porn sites they probably have begun by accident; the people who run these sites can be unscrupulous. For example after Princess Diana's death in 1997 a number of porn sites used her name so that people were directed to an innocent-looking web-site that turned out to be extremely unhealthy.

There is a mass of internet protection software on the market but we would recommend 'Covenant Eyes'. It is not difficult to use and will never clog up your system. The concept is very simple: it constantly monitors your computer and alerts an 'accountability partner' of your choice if you have looked at unhealthy web-sites. Each week your accountability partner will receive a report of your internet activity and if you were to look at something that was clearly a porn site they would be told – via e mail – immediately. We have used this in our home for some time and have found it invaluable. It can be installed on as many PC's as you have in your home and you could set yourself up as an 'accountability partner' for your children. Another way you could use it would be to ask them if they would consider their youth leader to partner with them; this will give them a sense of independence from you whilst keeping them accountable to another person. To demonstrate that you do not consider yourself immune from this danger you could make your teenage child one of your accountability partners. This will show your willingness for complete openness and sincerity. You can find more information at www.covenanteyes.com.

The Vanishing Car

The greatest act of trust is when a parent hands over their car keys to a newly-qualified teenage driver. Insurance costs will rocket, the car will disappear when you need it most, new dents and scratches will materialize and you may be barraged with angry words when you refuse to allow them take your car on a long distance drive. If you are going to let them use your car be prepared for an emotive source of tension to erupt in your home when you least expect it. This can be reduced by giving them a sense of responsibility in asking them to clean the car and pay for mileage (no matter how low this might be, it will re-enforce the fact that the car is on loan) and only allowing the car to be used by prior arrangement. The most damaging thing is to begin by letting them use it without question and then tightening the arrangement when you begin to feel uncomfortable.

Boy meets girl

When your son or daughter tells you that they have started dating you will find yourself in uncharted territory and will need to adapt very quickly. If your children have not come to this stage yet be careful not to tease them if they show an interest in someone of the opposite sex. You may find it amusing but to a young person it is humiliating and embarrassing and will only create more barriers between the two of you. Treat the relationship as a friendship until you are sure there is another aspect to it. Always set clear boundaries on where they are to go in the house and what time you expect them back, but be careful not to jump to conclusions about what they may be up to. A couple we know were sitting at home one spring evening talking about their wedding plans. They were so engrossed in their conversation that they did not notice dusk had fallen. When the young lady's mother came into the room she switched the light on and said 'men love darkness rather than light because their deeds are evil.' The couple concerned were married over fifty years ago but they still tell the story!

When your son or daughter and the person they are dating gaze endlessly into each others eyes try not to forget that you were once like them. A couple of decades into marriage can make you prone to forget what it was like. It would be helpful to recall times when you felt misunderstood by your parents this will enable you to understand the joys and heartaches your daughter or son is going through.

Breaking up is hard to do

You have watched the news and are just about to turn in for the night when your daughter arrives home early with a crest-fallen look on her face. You only need to look at her to know what it means. 'Mum,' she says through a salvo of sobs, 'we split up.' What do you say to a daughter or a son whose heart has been broken? The answer is: as little as possible; just be there for them and avoid platitudes. Never say 'I thought this would happen' or 'I never really liked him/her anyway' just show them that you love them and give them as much time as you can. These phases can be heart-wrenching for parents but if you show a genuine concern this can strengthen the bond between you and remind your son or daughter that they can always turn to you.

Practical Principles

It is no surprise that the list of problems parents face in the teenage years is the longest. We have tried to suggest ways of resolving them as we have gone along but here are some more general principles to help you through this challenging stage of parenting.

Show some respect

No, that is not a misprint! While 'respect' is a word not readily associated with teenagers one of the things they often struggle with is their self image and their place in the world. There is nothing more destructive for a relationship than to have a parent constantly criticising their dress-sense and attacking their musical tastes. You may not be a fan of heavy metal but it will mean a lot to your son or daughter if you take an interest in the music they listen to (although they may not admit to this). Try tuning in to their favourite music station and reading magazines reflecting teenage culture. It will help you understand their mindset and identify the issues they struggle with. Simon has been fortunate that his tastes in music are similar to our sons and he has enjoyed exchanging CD's and finding news about the latest releases. There have been times when he has even known something before they have! When they were teenagers our boys did not make a lot of comment on this but now they are older they seem quite proud of the way their dad has kept up with their culture. When Simon visited our youngest son he got talking to his flat-mates about music. After he had gone home they remarked how 'cool' his tastes were. However Matt was quick to add that they weren't impressed with Simon's fashion sense; you can't win them all!

A zealous but misdirected Christian father was very pleased with himself when he confiscated a CD his son had bought, gave him the money he paid for it and then threw it in the bin. 'I just had to make a stand' he proudly said as if he had confiscated drugs from him. His Pastor suggested a more positive way which would build bridges with his son: 'try sitting down and listening to it with him so that you can talk about the lyrics. Then you can help him understand the message the songs are communicating and compare them with what the Bible says.' This was too much of a compromise for such a pious man and he would have none of it. A few months later the young man rebelled against his father's values in a very destructive way.

Give them space

Although it is a fine balance to achieve, you need to be aware of what your teenage children are doing whilst giving them space to explore their growing independence. This does not come very easily to parents because we are used to protecting them and looking out for their interests. They will get hurt, make mistakes and suffer broken hearts but this is all part of growing up. Just be sure to be there when they need you and take action when there are signs of practices that could do them long-term harm such as drug or alcohol abuse and gently remind them of the standards God lays down for us in his Word.

Be nice to their friends

'Son, when are you going to get a nice friend?' That says two negative things to a teenager: firstly he does not find it easy to make friends and secondly those he has are no good. There was a day when you had some influence over their choices but that has long since past. The best thing you can do is to be nice to their friends and welcome them into your home. One of our sons used to invite a whole group over to our home every weekend to watch DVDs. We were fortunate that we had two rooms so we could let them use one and take refuge in the other and whilst at times it could be a little inconvenient it was good to know what they were doing without giving the appearance of interfering.

When your child takes his or her first steps into adolescence, parenting enters into its most challenging phase. Keep calm – it will not last forever and whilst it can be difficult there are many times when it is fun to have teenagers in the house. This will be a time when you can help your child make the transition into adulthood and learn more about yourself. See it as a season of opportunity.

Family life never quite fits the idealistic images you see on adverts, films and even on the cover of Christian magazines! There will be times when it seems as if war has broken out under your roof. Although this can be very difficult it is also an opportunity to see God do great things in your family and for you to grow in your relationship with him.

NOT QUITE EQUALLY YOKED

As a young man David was full of enthusiasm and zeal for the Lord. He was preaching in the open air every Saturday morning, doing one-to-one Bible studies with young men during the week and avidly reading good Christian literature at every possible opportunity. He started going out with Stacey who was part of the open air evangelism team and when they got married a year later everyone remarked at what potential two such keen Christians had in their work for the Lord. The first few years of their marriage were a whirlwind of Christian work: holidays were spent on Christian camps and their home was a haven to the young people. David was doing very well at his job and had some important promotions. Although he did not backslide or get involved in wrong practices David's love for God grew cold and put most of his energy into his job. Stacey however never lost her spiritual fire and suddenly found that she was not quite equally yoked to her husband.

Cindy and Liam were two of the most popular people in the youth group and when they started going out together they drew a big crowd around them. Rather than bask in their pooled popularity they decided to use it for God's Kingdom: Liam spent a lot of time coming alongside the young men to encourage them in their Christian life while Cindy did the same with the girls. They seemed so natural in Christian work that it was no surprise that they soon got married and continued their ministry by opening their home up to an expanding group. Lots of young people were strengthened and helped in their Christian lives and many were led to Christ and discipled during the next few years. Things slowed down when Cindy had a baby. They were so excited about the prospect of this new addition and they made some ambitious plans as to how they could extend their ministry by reaching out to families. After a beautiful baby girl was born Cindy started to behave quite out of character: she was withdrawn and tearful finding it even difficult to talk to Liam about it. They decided to consult the doctor and were told that Cindy had severe post-natal depression. They could not quite believe what they were hearing. Cindy had always been a bright and breezy girl with a positive outlook on life but now she seemed to have crawled into a shell. This went on for some months but she eventually came out of her depression and began to enjoy the challenges of motherhood. One thing however, changed: she never seemed to regain the spiritual fervour that she used to have. Liam tried reading the Bible with her, playing tapes of sermons that used to get her motivated to live for God and bought her Christian books he thought might help; but nothing worked. Cindy did not forsake her faith or stop going to Church (she even attended a mum's Bible study group) but she lost the joy and zeal she used to have. Liam, however, still longed for the activity and spiritual fervour of the old days.

Although both those couples are fictitious, in twenty years of ministry together we have seen similar circumstances many times. Whilst it seems more common for a husband to grow cold while his wife goes on with God it can happen to either party. This can lead to tensions and big mis-understandings within a relationship so it must be handled very sensitively.

Many of us have been rightly taught by Pastors and youth leaders that we must not become 'unequally yoked' by marrying someone who is not a Christian. But what if your spouse has grown cold in their relationship with the Lord?

Basic facts

Before we address this issue it is important to remember some fundamental facts from God's Word.

Fact one: you are in it for the long-haul

On the day you stood at the front of the church in view of your family and friends and made those awesome promises to each other, you said that you would be together 'for better or for worse' and 'in sickness and in health.' While you may have been prepared for the possibility of nursing your spouse through a serious illness or facing difficult circumstances together you may have not anticipated this particular problem. Nevertheless the vows you made before God and the Bible's teaching about marriage require you to stay committed to your marriage partner. This might sound obvious but we have known very sad situations where the more 'spiritual' partner begins to confide in someone of the opposite sex and after a time the deceitfulness of sin creeps in and an unhealthy bond develops between them. While that may seem remotely removed from your situation you must remember that no-one is immune from this and that it can happen very subtly. It will do no harm to be proactive by reminding yourself of your marriage commitment and to only confide in someone of the same sex. Also watch your relationship with your co-workers of the opposite sex in church activities: this is a dangerous area at such a time.

Fact two: only God creates spiritual fire

When a religious leader crept out under the cover of darkness to speak to Jesus about the Kingdom of God he got more than he expected. Jesus told him that 'no-one can see the kingdom of God unless he is born again' (John 3:3).

You can tell people the Good News about Jesus and a preacher can present a powerful message urging them to come to Christ but the it is the

Holy Spirit who opens their eyes to the truth and gives them new life. Paul reminded the Christians in Thessalonica of this when he said 'our gospel came to you not simply with words, but also with power, with the Holy Spirit and with deep conviction' (Thessalonians 1:5). In the same way you can pray for your partner and encourage them to get back to the place where they used to be, but only God can do a work in their heart. Sometimes you may be confused or even angry that it hasn't happened yet but you will have to trust God to do his work in his own time.

Fact three: God will finish what he started

Have you ever met someone who never seems to complete a task? Usually his house is strewn with tools left beside little jobs that he hasn't quite finished yet. The best kind of workman is one who begins a job and sticks at it until the last task has been fulfilled and the mess is cleared up. You will not care how long it takes him because you know that he will finish what he started. When Paul sat in a Roman prison he wrote to a group of Christians living in the Greek City of Philippi. He had been visited by one of their leaders who had brought news of the joys and sorrows of the Christian community there. At the very beginning of the letter Paul cited the things he thanked God for whenever these believers came to mind:'I am convinced' he said, 'That he who began a good work in you will carry it on to completion until the day of Christ Jesus' (Phil 1:6). God will not leave the work he started in your husband or wife unfinished. He may have allowed him or her to go through a period of spiritual decline but he still has his hand on them and will bring them safely across the threshold of heaven.

Let's go back to the two couples we met at the beginning of the chapter. Stacey has become quite frustrated with her husband's spiritual condition. She has tried the subtle approach: things like leaving Bibles around the house and playing Christian music on the stereo when he arrives home from work. On Sundays she has tried to bring up things in the sermon that seem relevant to David. However, he tidies the Bibles away, turns the stereo off and nods politely at her comments about the sermons. Stacey decides to try a more direct approach and starts saying things like, 'Why can't you be the way you were when we first got married?' David's defences instantly go up and he has a very anxious look on his face: 'What do you mean,' he asks nervously, 'are you suggesting that we have got troubles in our marriage?' She puts a hand on his shoulders and gives him a re-assuring smile, 'Of course not, I love you as much, if not more, than I did on the day I married you. I'm talking about your walk with the Lord.' David's whole posture changes, 'Oh that! Don't worry; it is all under control I haven't backslidden or anything.' Over the course of the next few months Stacey gives what she considers to be gentle encouragements reminding him to have his quiet time and challenging him about his prayer life. Eventually David snaps and says, 'Stacey, just get off my back! I've got enough pressure at work and I can do without your constant nagging.'

Stacey was right to be concerned for her husband's spiritual condition and had the best of motives in trying to encourage him but what she regarded as exhortation he perceived to be nagging. Her best course of action would be to do her utmost to be a godly wife and mother, pray for her husband and encourage him to pray with their children and read Bible stories to them.

Liam is very pleased that Cindy has become friendly with a young mum called Jackie. Jackie is a very outgoing, positive woman and despite having young children is very active in Christian work. Liam is hoping that this will influence Cindy and bring her back to the kind of person she used to be. After six months nothing seems to have changed and one day when he is tired and his defences are down Liam says, 'why can't you be like Jackie?' Unfortunately Cindy completely misunderstands him and bursts into tears; in between some desperate sobs she says, 'you don't love me any more.' Liam is a bit confused by this, 'Why on earth do you say that?' He says as he puts his arm around her and after a few minutes Cindy dries her eyes and replies, 'but all you've been talking about lately is Jackie; I thought you had started developing feelings for her.' Comparing your spouse to another person is a hurtful thing to do and it also carries the danger of being completely misunderstood. Do not even consider it – even in the quietness of your own thoughts - and if you ever make the mistake of making such a comparison apologise for it immediately.

Being not quite equally yoked can be a source of many little tensions which, if left unchecked, could lead you into serious dangers. It can cause heartache and will require you to tread very carefully and sensitively. Always keep in mind that this is not the end of the matter; God is at work and he will finish what he has begun.

THE EMPTY NEST

The day we watched our youngest son leave home will always be etched on our memory: his car was packed full and his spirits were soaring in anticipation of a new and exciting life ahead of him at university. Our hearts however were sinking by the second. After sharing a hug with him we closed the door and realised that from now on it would be just the two of us.

Nothing can prepare you for the trauma of seeing the last child 'fly the nest'; we cannot pretend that it is an easy time but it is a phase in which your relationship with your husband or wife can deepen and when you have a new bond with your son or daughter.

In the first few days of the 'empty nest' the silence hit us; there was no music from upstairs or sounds of late-night conversations on the mobile. We never realised how quiet we were. The house became unusually tidy too; believe it or not Simon actually missed coming downstairs and picking up the cushions that had been scattered around the floor and collecting up plates from various parts of the lounge. We cannot claim that it was an easy transition or that we did not miss Matt terribly but if you are about to go through this yourself we can promise that it does get easier and that it has its own benefits. The first question on your mind will be: 'how can I face this?' Here is some advice that we have gleaned from our experience.

Don't fight the emotions

When Simon was preaching at a church in Mobile Alabama the Pastor, who is one of his closest friends, took him on a drive to show him how the area was affected by Hurricane Katrina in 2006. The devastation was horrendous: houses levelled by the winds and huge trees ripped from their roots but those that were able to bend with the wind survived. The people who struggle the most when the nest becomes empty are those who fight or suppress the emotions that come with it. There is nothing wrong with feeling a sense of loss when your last child leaves home. You have finished an important chapter in your life and the constant access you had to him or her is no longer possible. You will feel sorrow, regret about the times you did not make the most of their company, and even a little bit of jealousy that they are beginning a new exciting life whilst you have the same old routine. One of the worst aspects for us was coming home to an empty house. These are natural reactions so go easy on yourself and let them run their course. The important thing is that whilst you acknowledge them, you do not let them rule your life.

Let go

Being a parent is a process of letting go from the moment you watch them take their first steps to the day they leave home. Simon's friend sent him a song that helped him come to terms with letting go. It was recorded by a group called '38 Special' and was originally written in a boy-meets-girl context but some of the lines are very appropriate for the empty nest:

> 'Just hold on loosely, but do not let go
> If you cling to tightly, you are gonna lose control'

We put that principle into practice and found that when we let our sons go they soon came back to us and we enjoyed an even better relationship than we had before. Roles are sometimes reversed: Matt drives Simon to the airport and gives him accommodation at his flat which makes this new phase even more special. Andrew our eldest son is married with a young child and we were overjoyed when they said they wanted to go away on holiday with us and living locally we often look after our grandson. The only downside is the feeling of getting on in years!

Keep in touch

When our youngest son started university the days of being dependent on the phone for communication were passed. We enjoyed talking with Matt on MSN Messenger and Skype and this made it less intrusive for him. We tried to respect his desire to be independent but take an interest in his course and his domestic arrangements. We were amazed to find out what a great cook he has become! The most heartening thing for us was talking to him about the church he had got involved in and listening to some of the preaching online.

Develop new interests

We have invested a lot of time in our family and we do not regret a second of it. However when the children grew up many of the things we used to do were no longer possible so we needed to develop some new interests for the time on our hands. We joined a gym, took walks in the countryside and travelled together more for ministry appointments. Make sure there are things you do together instead of using the bulk of your leisure time in a personal pursuit like playing golf or shopping.

There is no denying that it can be a heart-breaking point in a parent-child relationship but beyond it there is the joy of a completely new bond with your child – so hang on in there!

Chapter Two

Hiccups at church

ONE OF the most leading questions to ask a person is how things are going in their church. Some will wear a glowing smile and give you a detailed list of all the blessings they are enjoying and conversions they have seen while others will drop their head, sigh out loud, and say 'we've got problems.' Simon has been in Pastoral Ministry for two decades and in that time he has noticed how all churches seem to go through cycles: there are times when there is much to be encouraged about because God is blessing the work, periods when things seem to plateau and seasons when problems threaten to overwhelm. The kind of difficulties that are common during times like this will probably not affect you as intensely as they will pastor or a church leader but they can have a negative effect on spiritual life. This section is not a remedy for the troubles that can affect the local church but it will give you some simple principles to get through them with your spiritual life and your sanity intact.

BAD-MEETING BLUES

As you left the Sunday service you were handed an agenda for the next church business meeting. You glanced at it before you turned the ignition key in your car and it did not seem that it would be a particularly controversial meeting. The members were going to discuss the possibility of purchasing some new chairs for the main worship area and after sitting on those hard pews for an hour and a half it seemed like an excellent idea to you.

A few days later you arrived at the meeting expecting to be home by nine-thirty. The chairman opened with a short devotional talk and various Church Officers gave updates on projects they were involved in. As the item about the chairs approached you noticed that Mr. Bond, who was sitting close to you, started to shuffle in his seat and rustle his papers. The chairman told everyone about the rationale for replacing the pews: they were uncomfortable and unwelcoming for new people who have no church background. As soon as has he had finished Mr. Bond jumped to his feet and demanded to be heard. From the look on the chairman's face you could tell that he did not expect it to be helpful. 'Go ahead Percy,' he said (appearing to brace himself for an unpleasant experience). Mr. Bond was wearing a sober look on his face. 'I have been a member of this church for the last 30 years. These pews have seen us through times of great blessing and they have never put off anyone from attending this place of worship. What is more the Bible warns us about the kind of compromise you are proposing.' He waved his Bible at the chairman as if he was brandishing an armed weapon and flicked the pages until he came to the verse he was looking for, 'listen to what the Word of God says about this.' The atmosphere was electric; people sat on the edge of their seats wondering what the Bible could possibly say about pews. With a triumphant tone in his voice Mr. Bond read from the Prophet Amos and said 'woe to those who are at ease in Zion' (Amos 6:1 ESV), then he turned to Revelation citing the verse that says 'because you are lukewarm – neither hot nor cold – I am about to spit you out of my mouth' (Rev 3:16). He slammed his Bible shut, pointed it at the chairman and sternly said 'If we replace those pews with cushy chairs we will betray our heritage. The blessings God has given us over the years will disappear as we relax in our new-found comfort and ease.' He sat down and the chairman prepared to reply but before he was able to open his mouth Mrs. Bentley got to her feet. She told the meeting that as 'the Senior Member' her opinions should be listened to and no-one had consulted her about this matter. 'I agree wholeheartedly with Mr. Bond and what is more – we have the Word of God on our side!' The meeting seemed to descend into freefall with arguments and recriminations shooting across the room and it eventually drew to a close at ten-thirty without the issue being resolved. Before you left the meeting you said a few comforting words to the chairman and walked out of the building wondering what the fuss was all about.

If you have been a member of a church it is likely that you have experienced such a meeting. Churches are full of sinners who have been forgiven and since they are yet to be made perfect their sin will seep out. What better forum than a church business meeting! The most potent thing about them is the surprise factor: major issues often go through with little tension and wide agreement but small, seemingly insignificant items can blow up into full-scale battles.

Take a break

If the meeting has gone on late you will want to throw yourself into bed and try to pretend that it has never happened. If you do so there is one thing you can be sure of – you will not sleep very well. As soon as your head hits the pillow Mr. Bond will start waving his Bible at you and Mrs. Bentley will be reminding you that she is the 'Senior Member.' Although it is late it would be better for you to do something to take your mind off the difficult evening you have just had. After committing the whole thing to the Lord in prayer try watching the comedy program you have recorded or reading a few chapters of a light book or listening to some relaxing music with a warm drink in your hands. It will give you much more chance of a good nights sleep.

One of the things that helped to preserve Simon's sanity in his years as a pastor is a sense of humour. One day you will look back on this meeting and laugh; so why not do it now? Mr. Bond may have caused a little bit of havoc but he has shown that his skills in handling the Bible need a lot of work. If you find the scene replaying in your mind try to see the funny side of it and it will seem very different to you.

Attitude is everything

No-one can argue with the fact that you have just experienced a very unpleasant meeting and you will be right to feel a little angry about it. We have already made note of the warnings the Bible gives us to ensure that the 'sun does not go down on your wrath' (Eph 4:26) and that, 'man's anger does not lead to the righteous life that God requires' (James 1:20). If you let your anger continue unchecked you will find it quite difficult to enter into the next worship service. Be careful not to develop a negative attitude towards people like Mr. Bond and Mrs. Bentley; you can counter this by thanking God for their good points. If this is the only difficult meeting in a church that has known a lot of blessing and encouragement see it in perspective and pray that God would give the leaders wisdom to resolve the issue. And be sure to keep friendly with everyone involved.

No sides

In our experience it is very rare for churches to divide on important issues. Controversies in business meetings usually revolve around issues such as seats, hymn books and the colour the building should be decorated. If a meeting you have attended has exploded into a row over such a matter make sure that you do not take sides, so you will be in a position to help people get things into perspective. You could have a talk with Mr. Bond and ask him to explain why this issue is so important to him and find out if there is a compromise he would be willing to reach. Be clear that you are not acting on anybody's behalf but you are just concerned that the church does not split over an issue that will have no consequence in the long term. Assure him of your prayers and your ongoing love and respect. If you do the same with people on the other side of the dispute you could be a catalyst for change.

Analysis paralysis

A meeting such as the one you have just experienced does not really end when the chairman has closed in prayer; it will be endlessly discussed and analyzed for weeks to come. Statements that have been made and body language that was adopted will be put under intense scrutiny. The tendency will be to keep coming back to the problem without looking for a solution. If you find a conversation you are having begins to drift in that direction do everything you can to change it. You could bring up something else to talk about, or if you feel comfortable enough to do so, question whether it is productive to talk about such things. If you do, make sure that you avoid sounding remotely self-righteous. Try something like this: 'one of the verses that has helped me in the past is Philippians 4:8 "whatever is true, whatever is noble, whatever is right, whatever is pure, whatever is lovely, whatever is admirable—if anything is excellent or praiseworthy—think about such things." It really challenged the way I kept going over things like this in my mind and it stopped me from bringing them up in conversations.'

Three months later you may attend the next meeting with a sense of trepidation but go with a positive attitude. It is very likely that in the intervening time your leaders will have been working hard to bring the church to unity over this issue. Every church will have a case of 'bad meeting blues' at some time or another but since the issues are rarely anything of great consequence over time they are usually resolved. Remember: in a years time you may be even be chuckling about it!

A HOUSE DIVIDED

Louise had just begun a new job which involved her moving house and leaving the church she had been part of for the last six years. She had spent time searching the internet for suitable churches and eventually found somewhere that seemed ideal. As she pulled into the car park she was encouraged with the modern building and liked the sound of the music group playing. However a few things unsettled her: as she walked in she noticed a group of people huddled together in such an intense discussion that they did not even notice her. There seemed to be a strained atmosphere hanging over the service and the Pastor looked tense and punctuated his sermon with comments about disunity and gossip (even though they had nothing to do with the passage he was preaching on). When the service closed most people talked in groups and the tone of their conversation did not appear to be small talk. Few people spoke to her and the Pastor did not seem very excited to have a potential new member of the congregation. As she got into her car and drove home she reflected on the experience and realised that the church appeared to be riddled with bad feeling and division and she decided not to settle there.

When division is allowed to fester in a church it will draw more and more people into its web. As Louise was a visitor she was able to walk away from it but that is not always possible, or advisable if it is happening in the church family you are committed to. In the following paragraphs we set out some principles which will enable you to avoid getting caught up in division and take steps to help resolve it.

Question people's claims

People are prone to exaggerate – especially if they are caught up in a situation like the one just described. We have even known people to label a difference of opinion in their fellowship as 'a blood bath'! When this happens, question the kind of phrases they are using. There may have been raised voices and unkind words but no blood has been spilt. When you challenge these claims it will help people put things into perspective; a 'blood bath' is something that cannot be resolved but a difference of opinion or a personality conflict, with the help and enabling of God's Spirit, can be overcome.

PERSONALITY ISSUES

John, Tim and Julie often talked the night away over a cup of coffee; on this occasion they had got into a heated discussion about their favourite preachers. John was enthusing about Ron Macdonald 'I think he is God's man for the hour. I came to Christ through his ministry and his teaching has helped me throughout my Christian life. I've got stacks of his books and CDs and there is not a dud one among them.' Whilst he says this Julie is vigorously shaking her head 'But he is yesterday's man, he was all right for the basics but you have got to move on to someone who can give you some deeper teaching. Try Roy Varney; now he is a man with his finger on the spiritual pulse of the nation. He can teach you things that you would never dream of knowing.' Tim is dismissive of both of them, 'You have obviously never listened to Stan Blakey, he's a dynamic preacher. Once you have heard him you will never want to listen to anyone else again.' Does that sound familiar to you? If you have not heard it for yourself you will have read about it in the Bible because the Christians in Corinth were dividing into different groups that were devoted to particular preachers and the apostle Paul was having none of it:

'My brothers, some from Chloe's household have informed me that there are quarrels among you. What I mean is this: One of you says, "I follow Paul"; another, "I follow Apollos"; another, "I follow Cephas"; still another, "I follow Christ." Is Christ divided? Was Paul crucified for you? Were you baptised into the name of Paul?' (1 Corinthians 1:11-13).

Division in churches often revolves around different personalities and some people will naturally have more attractive characteristics than others. Be careful that you do not get drawn to people; it is possible that they may be using their personal charisma to gather a faction around them. You should also be cautious about people who show concern about an issue you may have with one or all of the leaders of the church. You will usually find that this is a tactic to gather a critical mass of people around them so that they can claim they have backing for their own cause. They are like Absalom who after being banished from Jerusalem, stayed outside the city, listening to people's protests and problems saying, 'If only I were appointed judge in the land! Then everyone who has a complaint or case could come to me and I would see that he receives justice' and in doing this he 'stole the hearts of the people' (2 Samuel 15:4, 6).'

If you have a grievance do everything you can to keep it between you and the person concerned. You can be sure that once it gets out the wrong kind of people will get drawn in; they may give you attention and express concern for you but their aim is to cause trouble and to create division.

LEADERS AT LOGGERHEADS

It used to be a delight to see the church leaders walk out of the prayer room together before a service began; it was all smiles and laughter. More recently they've been emerging with grim looks on their faces and you have even wondered if you have noticed them glaring at one another. When leaders are at loggerheads the Church will inevitably lose its sense of direction and cracks in the unity will appear.

Tell them that you are praying for them and encourage them about the way in which their ministry has been a blessing to the church in past years. Express your concern that there appears to be some tension among the leadership but make sure that you do not pry. If it comes up in conversation with someone else turn the matter over to prayer.

HOW THE MIGHTY HAVE FALLEN

The local paper has dropped on the mat with news that makes your stomach turn: 'local Minister arrested on drug charges.' As soon as your eyes scan the headline you read through the sordid details that have been recounted with relish and no doubt a degree of embellishment to spice up the story.

'Minister Horatio Smith was stopped by Police on his way home from church last Sunday. As he got out of the car his eyes looked glazed and he argued with Police. Rev Smith has tested positive for drugs and was charged under the Abuse of Substance Act.'

Thankfully this kind of occurrence is very rare but when it does happen it is a huge source of disappointment and discouragement to everyone concerned and it can also cast a shadow over a local church that may take some time to disperse. The circumstances and specific sins may vary but sadly there is nothing new about the occasional but tragic fall of a leader. In the New Testament Peter and John Mark stumbled but found their way back, whereas Demas 'fell in love with this present world' (2 Tim 4:10) and Judas hung himself after betraying Jesus.

If a leader in your fellowship had to resign his position in disgrace you should expect some serious fall-out: people will be confused (particularly new Christians), his fellow-leaders will be stunned, and for a time, everyone will have a heavy heart.

Reactions

At a time like this your own reactions will need some careful attention. Here is the array of emotions you may experience:

Bewilderment

Somehow it does not seem possible that the Pastor you loved and trusted, who saw you through some difficult times could have done the very things he has preached against. There will be times when you think there may have been a mistake and that he has not actually committed the act he has confessed to. This is a natural reaction the mind unleashes as a self-protection mechanism enabling you to cope with the initial aftermath of the tragedy. Let it run its course.

Betrayal

You were at his induction service and remember him promising to 'care for the flock God had entrusted into his care.' And you ask yourself how he could desert you all for the sake of a practice that he knew to be wrong? Remember that Jesus was betrayed by someone he loved and trusted and he committed the matter into his Father's hands.

Doubt

Sometimes a fallen leader will deny everything he has preached about in order to pursue a lifestyle that he knows to be wrong. If you have benefited from his teaching and pastoral care for some years you may have niggling doubts about the things he taught you. Just remember that it is his character and not the Word of God that has been proved wanting. Hold onto anything you have been taught that stands up to the test of Scripture.

Realism

Be careful not to seize the moral high ground and look down on the man who has fallen. The Bible warns us, 'If you think you are standing firm, be careful that you do not fall!' (1 Corinthians 10:12). These sad circumstances are a wake up call for every Christian to examine himself or herself. Ask yourself 'am I careless with sin? Are there things going on in my life that I am complacent about?'

Hope

Jesus said 'I will build my Church and the gates of hell shall not prevail against it' (Matt 16:18). Throughout Church history there have been many sad cases of godly men falling into sin but it has never been destroyed by such problems. Take heart from the fact that the Lord Jesus will continue to build the local expression of his Church that you belong to.

PASTOR ON THE MOVE

It started off the same as any other Sunday. The music group played as people came in to take their seats, the Pastor welcomed everyone to the service and the church was full. Looking nervous and drawn he shuffled in the pulpit and pulled out a crumpled piece of paper from his pocket, you looked over to his wife and noticed that she was close to tears. Then he dropped his bombshell: 'Charlotte and I have enjoyed ten happy years in this church and we were looking forward to many more.' He paused to draw a deep breath and looked down at the floor, 'However the Lord seems to have other plans for our lives and I have accepted an invitation to be the Senior Minister of King's Street Baptist Church.' For a moment the congregation was so quiet that you could hear a pin drop; then one or two gasps of surprise could be heard. The Pastor then looked up and continued his announcement, 'I'm not leaving for another few months so let's enjoy the rest of the time we have together.' The children then left for their classes and the congregation stumbled through the next song in a state of shock. It might have been your imagination but it seemed as if after making that announcement he preached the best sermon you have ever heard from him.

Sad as it is at the time this kind of scenario is a lot healthier than the one we have just thought about. There has been no moral failure or public shame but you will have a sense of loss and even betrayal that the Pastor you have loved and trusted so long is moving to another church which, by all accounts, has more people and greater potential than your own. Having been in Christian ministry for some years we are in a position to be able to give you a glimpse of both sides.

Although you may congratulate him on his appointment you will certainly be feeling a little bit resentful that he is leaving you; especially if he has visited the other church on several occasions under a cloak of secrecy. Try to look at it from his perspective: he will probably have been approached by the leaders of this church and been surprised by the invitation. If he is anything like Simon, (who has been in a similar position) he may have been agonizing over his decision, reluctant to leave his present pastoral charge, but excited about the possibility of a fresh challenge. Go easy on him and try not to make him feel guilty about 'leaving you in the lurch.' When he has finally said goodbye, do not tell him how well you are doing without him; it may leave him questioning the effectiveness of his ministry with you! Enjoy the last few months that you have together and put the date of the induction at the new church in your diary as soon as it is announced. It will mean a lot to your Pastor and to his new church to have you there.

The first Sunday without him will undoubtedly seem very strange but the challenge of this time may bring out surprising gifts and abilities in people. Over the years the Pastor may have taken on many jobs and roles and you will be delighted to see the Lord raise up people who are able to take them on. The 'interregnum', as it is often called, need not be a dead space between the end of one ministry and the beginning of another but an exciting time of challenge for the church. Give your church leaders extra encouragement during this time.

AN UNFRIENDLY CHURCH

'That's me there in the corner
my head upon my hands, or maybe I'm the one who's trying to smile
and I'm the one reflected in the mirror on the wall
looking sad, but I'll be all right, I'll be all right, I'll be all right in a while.

I'm staring through the window at the rooftop and the light
thinking anywhere's the best place I could be
and I'm the one who's sitting at the table all alone
looking tired but I'll be all right, I'll be all right, I'll be all right; just wait and
see.

Glory hallelujah there's a lot of people singing
and I think I get the message about really being free,
and all this holding hands and saying you've got to love each other,
all this talk of Jesus but you didn't talk to me.

That's me there by the doorway, I've already said goodbye
or is that me there looking back there just one more time.
I'm the one who's kicking stones and walking in the rain
looking fine but I'll be all right by tomorrow I'll be fine

This song by Phil Thompson and Adrian Snell ingeniously reflects what
many of us experience when we visit a church for the first time. There is a buzz
of conversation and everyone is busy chatting in their little groups, but you
are ignored. What do you do when you find a church that has great teaching
but does not seem to be very welcoming to new people?

Look for someone else on their own

If it is a big church there may be other people visiting for the first time; they
will be easy enough to spot because no-one will be talking to them either!

Introduce yourself to them and see if you can team up to get to know people in the church.

Think about your body language

It may not be that people are ignoring you; they are probably shy and do not know how to strike up a conversation. Sometimes your body language can make you look a bit defensive. Be as relaxed as you can; try to get some eye contact with people and smile at them – it will work wonders.

Buttonhole the person at the door

Most churches have people on welcome duty at the door. Speak to one of them after the service and ask if they can introduce you to people of your own age. We know a young man who did this and was introduced to a girl who later became his wife - you never know what might happen!

Make a difference

The church you have visited may seem unfriendly but you could be the person God has brought there to make a difference. Try sticking with it and getting involved. Put welcoming new people at the top of your agenda.

THE QUIET CHRISTIAN

Ever since she was a young girl Kelly had thrived in the limelight. When she was little she was always the cute little girl at the front who stole the show, she was given the role of Mary in the Nativity play and she was the 'Prom Queen' when she was sixteen. By that description you would expect Kelly to have been a precocious young woman always looking into a mirror and preening her hair but she was actually nothing like that. She was very caring and if a girl her age came to the youth group for the first time she did everything possible to make her feel welcome. Kelly had a beautiful voice which the church Music Director regularly put to good use and she was involved in many high profile activities in the church.

Sarah had been Kelly's best friend from early childhood but she was more comfortable in the background. When she was very young she used to hide at the back during a public performance and at parties and socials she would be found sitting in the corner. Like Kelly, Sarah was a very gifted young woman: she had a wonderful ability to teach children and to keep their attention but she never pushed herself forward to take part in children's services or be at the front in the Kid's club. Since she was so quiet and Kelly so extrovert she was constantly passed over in favour of her friend despite the fact that she could probably have done a better job. It was not that people thought badly of her; she just never figured in their thinking. Sarah never complained but there were times when she felt frustrated and sometimes even a little resentful towards her friend. When she went to college she joined a small church and soon became involved in the children's work. People from her home church were amazed at the things she was able to do and asked why she had 'hidden her light under a bushel' for so many years. She would shrug her shoulders and say 'I guess it was because no-one ever asked me.'

We need extroverts in the local church. They are great at breaking the ice and making new people feel more comfortable and can be relied on to do something at the front when everyone else shrinks away from it. However, the situation we have just described underlines the danger of ignoring the quiet Christian who may be very gifted but is often passed over. If you are a youth leader or a church officer make sure that you do not overlook an unassuming person who is always ready to help with a job and faithful in attending meetings but never willing to put themselves forward. If you are the type of person I've just described what should you do to maximise your potential without pushing yourself forward?

Know what your gifts are

The first step is to discover the gifts the Lord has given you with which you can build up his church.

Here are three questions which will help to identify them.

• What am I effective at?

Sarah knew that she was effective in communicating with children. That is why, soon after she joined a church, she got involved in the children's work.

• What am I really passionate about?

If the Lord has given you a gift he will also give you the enthusiasm and passion to put it into practice.

• What do my Christian friends and my church leaders think I am gifted at?

This provides the checks and balances. No-one is infallible and you may think you have a gift when your church leaders and friends do not agree. If you find yourself disappointed with an answer they give, ask them to tell you what they think your gifts are and spend some time considering their answer and praying this through.

Break out

You may be a quiet, shy person but there comes a time when you need to break out of your shell and volunteer to do something. Do not sit back and think 'I could never do that'; you will not know until you have tried.

GOOD CHURCH – SHAME ABOUT THE PREACHING

Every Sunday morning the roads around Fifth Street Community Church are jammed with cars. It seems as if everyone in the town has heard about Tony Richards the dynamic young preacher who took up the Pastorate a few months ago. Several blocks down Mike Wardle preaches to a much smaller congregation at Montgomery Road Chapel. He shares the same evangelical convictions as Tony Richards but does not possess the communication skills of his ministerial neighbour.

Fifth Street Community Church is so large that it is easy to get lost in the crowd but at Montgomery Road Chapel you will be spotted and welcomed instantly. Imagine that after visiting both churches you decide to go to the smaller one so that you can make more of a contribution (which is a great approach to take). After a few months you have become very involved in the fellowship and built up some great friendships. You love the church but when the sermon begins your heart sinks. Rev. Wardle is faithful to the Bible and wonderful with people but you struggle to keep track of what he is saying and quietly breathe a sigh of relief as soon as he finishes and announces the last hymn.

If you identify with this, think about why you joined such a church in the first place. You will probably have been struck by its warmth and faithfulness and will have identified areas in which you could help. You may even have been to a large church before – like the one just described – and whilst you enjoyed everything about the service you walked out of the door without anyone welcoming you as a visitor. Over a period of time that will be forgotten so it would be a good thing to remind yourself of this fact.

Instead of focusing on the things you do not like about the preaching identify your Pastor's strengths, and thank God for them. Concentration on sermons becomes a lot easier if you take notes; whilst you are listening ask yourself 'what is God challenging me about?' and 'what is the main point I need to take home with me?' Then go over it in your quiet time the next morning. This will transform the way you think about the sermons and enrich your spiritual life. Remember to pray for your Pastor too.

HELP! I'M IN THE WRONG ROLE

It seemed like good idea at the time: the leaders of the Kid's Club were pleading for volunteers and you were available at the times they needed help the most. Ten months on you dread Wednesday evenings and struggle to do the simplest tasks you are given. As you walk up to the church you think 'this is just not me', when the club is on you feel like calling out 'Lord, please get me out of here' and it is a relief when you are finished.

You may have offered your help with the best of intentions but it has now become burdensome and you realise that you are in the wrong role. The first thing we want to remind anyone in this position is that you have not done anything wrong; in fact you have not even made a mistake. You have shown yourself willing to help wherever needed, tested your gifting and found that it does not lie in this particular area. So there is no need to feel embarrassed or ashamed. There is no point being 'a square peg in a round hole'. Your co-workers are probably aware that you are struggling to fulfil your responsibility but feel too awkward to tell you. Speak to the leaders as soon as possible and see if there are other areas of service in which it would be best for you to invest your time; you can use the three questions that were used earlier.

HOW CAN WE MANAGE WITHOUT THEM?

Lots of families are committed to the church they belong to. The husband and wife may lead youth work and run the cleaning team whilst their children play in the music group. We should be so thankful for people like this but the downside is that it can be a huge blow if they relocate and have to leave the church. They are involved in so many of the activities that you wonder whether the work can possibly continue without them.

In the classic British TV comedy program 'Dad's Army' when something went wrong a character called Corporal Jones used to run around the room shouting 'don't panic' and the result was more chaos and increased panic. The news that a key family is on the move (especially in a small church) can have the same effect, so the first thing to do when you hear it is to make sure that you do not push the panic button; no-one is irreplaceable. In two decades of ministry we have seen the most surprising people come out of the shadows to continue the work in these circumstances. Perhaps part of the reason the

Lord is moving them on is that you have become a little too dependent on them.

Remember that the local Church is the Lord's property; he cares about this problem and you should bring it to him holding onto the promise that he will 'supply all [our] needs according to his glorious riches in Christ Jesus' (Phil 4:19). Whilst you depend on God and look to him to fill the gap you must do everything you can to deal with the situation. After praying about it, list the areas they were involved in and determine the commitment required from those who will take on each role. Then you will know what needs to be done and will be able to communicate clearly to people in the church. There may be some jobs that could be shared by two or more people; which will make them seem more manageable to anyone who is considering volunteering. Remember the 'quiet Christian' we thought about earlier; God may be clearing a space so that he can move them into a job he wants them to do.

Make sure that in the busyness of allocating these jobs you express your care and concern for the family who are moving on. It is going go be very tough for them to leave their church and friends and start again. When some friends of ours - who were involved in many aspects of the life of their church - moved away, people insensitively told them how well things were going since they left. 'Don't worry about the church' they were told, 'We're doing fine without you.' This comment did not really help them adjust to their move and left them feeling a little hurt.

HOLDING THE FORT

At first you had a team working alongside you but in recent months it seems to have disintegrated. First Harry had to give up because of work commitments, then Sue moved to another area and finally you were the only one left.

You may try to carry on as long as you can but if you cannot continue the work on your own and desperately need some help, let people know. One word of caution: be careful not to play the martyr telling everyone that you are the only one left and that the church leaders have abandoned you. No matter how neglected you may feel this needs to be handled in an attitude of love and grace.

Sometimes a work continues much longer than it should, and depending on the nature of it, you must face the question as to whether it has run its natural course. It may be that God is doing a new thing and you have not quite caught up yet.

RELATIONSHIP ISSUES

The biggest difficulties in churches are relational. It is great when people get along with one another but when cracks appear in relationships all kinds of problems emerge. In this chapter we are going to look at some of the common hiccups caused by the way that Christians relate to one another.

Clash of co-workers

Rob and Alan shared a fervour for evangelism and they decided to form a small team to go out into the shopping precinct each Saturday to do some. Despite their common passion and complimentary gifts they often clashed. Rob was impulsive and untidy while Alan was organized and liked to feel that everything was under control. This was a continual source of friction between them until it erupted into a full scale argument in front of the rest of the team.

God has made us as individuals but in a fallen world this can lead to tension between Christians. The most difficult thing is when you have two workers – both gifted and committed to the work – who do not get on.

Most people see conflict as something negative but it is not always bad, in fact sometimes it is necessary. Proverbs says 'As iron sharpens iron, so one man sharpens another' (Prov 27:17). Jesus never shied away from conflict in his ministry: he faced the Pharisees up to their own sin, he warned Peter that he would betray him and he turned over the tables of the money changers. Some of his most significant teaching arose from tension with his opponents. Not only did Paul 'cross swords' with false teachers who tried to undermine his work but there were also times when he clashed with fellow workers such as Peter and Barnabas. The conflict with Peter led to a clarification of the important issue of Gentile believers being part of the church and the clash with Barnabas (over the disappointment they'd had at the conduct of John Mark) resulted in the two men going their separate ways. It is totally unrealistic to never expect conflict between co-workers; sometimes it has to emerge so that a new way forward can be forged from two opposite perspectives.

If you find yourself at loggerheads with a co-worker you will firstly need to deal with your own heart. The most harmful thing to do would be to spill out everything that has been swilling around in your thoughts. Memorise the following verse and bring it to mind every time you are tempted to tell someone what you think of them: 'A fool gives full vent to his anger, but a wise man keeps himself under control' (Proverbs 29:11). At this stage the safest thing to do is to talk to God. Get on your own, have an open Bible in front of you and tell him exactly what you feel. Although you might think you are in the right, remember you are a sinner saved by God's grace just like the other person and that there may be sin lurking in your heart. Acknowledge that fact to the Lord and pray David's prayer:

> 'Search me, O God, and know my heart; test me and know my anxious thoughts. See if there is any offensive way in me, and lead me in the way everlasting' (Psalm 139:23-24)

Confess any sins he brings to mind and ask him to help you to forgive your co-worker for the things that have irritated or angered you. And remember that forgiveness is not a feeling: it is an act of obedience.

Having worked through this, identify the issue that has caused the problem and ask God to give you the wisdom needed to address it with him or her. Remember that the New Testament says that 'if any of you lacks wisdom he should ask God who gives generously to all without finding fault and it will be given to him'. (James 1:5). That is another great verse to memorise! Once you have done this seek to meet up with them in a relaxed environment to talk about the issues that have led to this conflict. Chip Ingram has taught that vulnerability builds bridges but anger creates distance. This is an important principle which will help to resolve this problem. Lay some of the blame on the way that you have perceived the issue and it is likely that the other person will open up. Always see yourself as part of the problem and be ready to listen to the other person's point of view.

Stress that it is important that you get along for the sake of the Lord's work. Simon's brother-in-law, who used to be a Royal Marine, described the way he had to spend the night in a fox hole with some of his comrades. Simon asked him if there were times when they used to argue and irritate each other. David knowingly shook his head and said 'that is something we were always taught to avoid because our lives depended on one another. We had to get on!' If this conflict is allowed to continue it will escalate and could completely undermine the work you are both committed to. Neither of you want that.

After you have sorted things out between you set some ground rules to ensure that this does not happen again. This could include regular prayer together, clearing up misunderstandings as soon as they arise, trying to see things from one another's point of view and never doing anything to undermine one another.

If you are leading a work in which other people are clashing deal with it as early as possible: it will only fester if it is left. Get each of them alone and urge them to follow the steps we have just thought about. If they do not feel comfortable with this, get them together but set some important rules for the meeting: they must not insult or blame each other, they should listen to what the other person has to say and their aim must be to resolve the issues that are at the heart of the problem.

One word of warning: never send e mails out in this kind of situation. They are prone to misinterpretation and are often the cause of a lot of unnecessary misunderstanding.

A romance ends

For two years it seemed as if they were joined at the hip. They shared a hymn book so they could hold hands and during the service they would glance at each other and exchange soppy smiles. Everyone thought that the announcement of their engagement was imminent but one Sunday they came into church separately and sat at opposite sides of the building. She spent the time sobbing whilst he would not look at anything except the floor.

Those of us who are older have probably experienced the end of a romance. Our experience assures us that in time the people involved will get over it. However the initial fall-out can make life difficult for everyone around them too. It has the danger of dividing the young people and it may be a source of gossip for the next few weeks.

For the last two years these two young people's lives have been bound together; they have had a shared identity and now they are individuals again. This is going to make it very difficult for them to even walk into the church or into the Youth Leader's home when the group is meeting. Do everything you can to make each of them feel comfortable and welcome.

It may be helpful for a youth leader or another mature Christian to spend time talking things through with them and this should naturally be male to male and female to female.

There will probably be awkwardness between them for some time but they will both need help in adjusting to a different - and for a time painful - relationship with one another. They need to be able to look one another in the eye and communicate, albeit in a very limited way. Try to encourage each of them to see that this will actually help them begin to get over the break-up although it will take some time.

Be careful not to deluge them with platitudes - they are rarely helpful. These young people do not want to know that there are 'plenty more pebbles on the beach' or that 'time heals'; they just want to get through the day in one piece emotionally. In the initial days and weeks after the break-up just be there for them and let them grieve over the loss of a relationship.

Try to put yourself in their position; they will be feeling vulnerable and hurt. When the break up is the decision of one person, the other party will be left feeling more hurt but even if it is a shared decision, it can still be painful for both.

As a youth leader (or church leader), praying for wisdom to ask the right questions will help you to gently guide them through the healing process (see James 1:5 and 3:17-18).

If they have been involved in a sphere of service together talk to them about what they would like to do and how you can help make things less awkward for them. This may be the time for a new field of minstry; it would certainly help them to look outside of themselves and give them something else to focus on.

Some of their peers may engage in fevered gossip and speculation about the situation and others may even be positioning themselves to be the next boyfriend or girlfriend. The challenge for a youth leader will be to put a stop to this and urge the whole group to support them both. The last thing they need is to be the source of gossip or to jump into a new romance.

Business fall-out

It is always sad when you hear someone say 'never do business with a Christian', because they have been let down or treated badly. Christians should be the very best people to deal with in business because of their honesty and integrity. The most difficult thing is when people within a church have been in business together and something goes wrong.

Business disputes sometimes end up in court but this is something that as Christians we must avoid. Remember the clear instructions given in the New Testament:

> 'If any of you has a dispute with another, dare he take it before the ungodly for judgment instead of before the saints? Do you not know that the saints will judge the world? And if you are to judge the world, are you not competent to judge trivial cases? Do

you not know that we will judge angels? How much more the things of this life! Therefore, if you have disputes about such matters, appoint as judges even men of little account in the church! I say this to shame you. Is it possible that there is nobody among you wise enough to judge a dispute between believers? But instead, one brother goes to law against another—and this in front of unbelievers! The very fact that you have lawsuits among you means you have been completely defeated already. Why not rather be wronged? Why not rather be cheated? Instead, you yourselves cheat and do wrong, and you do this to your brothers' (1 Corinthians 6:1-8).

If you find yourself in this situation ask your church leader or a mature Christian with business experience to mediate and agree to abide by what they recommend. You may feel that you lose out in the short term but God will be glorified and he will honour the way you have handled this. As far as possible this should be kept amongst those directly affected because if it leaks out it could divide the church making it more difficult to resolve.

Business disputes within a local church have the potential to spill over and cause many problems. Here are some steps you can take to prevent this.

Avoid exaggerated language

You may be tempted to say, 'he ruined my businesses' or, 'she has wrecked my life,' but stop and ask yourself if that is really true. If God were to ask you to give a description of what had happened how would you describe it to him? Remember that he knows everything that has happened and what is going on in the hearts of everyone involved in the dispute.

See it in the light of eternity

In the magnificent chapter about love in 1 Corinthians, Paul looked forward to what lies ahead of us in heaven saying, 'when perfection comes, the imperfect disappears' (1 Cor 13:10). And after this he draws an example from his own experience.

> 'When I was a child, I talked like a child, I thought like a child, I reasoned like a child. When I became a man, I put childish ways behind me. Now we see but a poor reflection as in a mirror; then we shall see face to face. Now I know in part; then I shall know fully, even as I am fully known.' 1 Corinthians 13:10-12 (NIV)

When he was a boy Simon was the proud owner of a 'Space Hopper'. For those who do not know, this was a big plastic ball with handles (made to look like ears) to hold onto. The idea was to sit on it and hop – or bounce – wherever you wanted to go. Simon decided to ride his Hopper to a shop a couple of blocks away and so a journey that would have taken ten minutes took the best part of an hour. When he eventually arrived home him mum was anxiously waiting outside for him, 'where have you been? I've been so worried about you! And you've missed your favourite programme "Bugs Bunny". As soon as he heard this Simon sulked for the next hour. This was before the days of DVD recorders and as far as he was concerned that episode of his favourite program was lost for ever.

That was a long time ago, and now that Simon is an adult the things that were upsetting to him as a child are insignificant. Similarly when we get to heaven the difficulties we have been concerned about here will be forgotten. So why not let some of that heavenly light into the situation you face now?

We know from personal experience that these problems can seem very difficult to surmount but remember 'nothing is impossible with God'. He can work a miracle when you least expect it.

'I've been hurt – yes I've been hurt'

Now this really dates us but we associate those words with the British Pop group 'Gary Pucket and the Union Gap'. The song is all about the break up of a relationship but there have been many times when we can identify with the refrain.

> 'I've been hurt, hurt, hurt
> Yes I've been hurt
> I've been hurt like I've never been hurt before'

People can say or do things that make you feel as if a knife has been stuck in your chest and sometimes Christians can be the worst offenders. Someone once said: 'Christians are the only people who shoot their wounded.'

A friend of ours who has been a Pastor for many years says, 'it is a pity that some Christians like to give you a piece of their mind because when they do there is not usually much in them in the first place.' We have lost count of the number of 'off-the-cuff' comments that have caused hurt and offence. Having led a service for the first time a young man stands at the door and is told off about his bad use of English grammar. A joke about height or appearance is made at someone else's expense. A teenager is told that he is 'evil' because he likes to listen to rock music. Such comments may be said in jest but they can wound. What do you do if you are on the receiving end?

Rather than pretend you are not hurt acknowledge it to yourself and talk to God about it. You may have told yourself that it was only a joke or a passing comment that does not matter but when you bury a hurt it can fester and anger may start to seep out. It may be helpful to have a quiet word with the person concerned and explain how you feel. However make sure that you approach them in a spirit of reconciliation so that 'whatever you do, you do in love' (1 Cor 16:14). They may be pleased that you have pointed this out and dismayed that you have been offended by their words.

Emotions are not bad but they can be tyrants if you allow them to rule your life. Try to prevent them from shaping your thoughts and actions; this is an effective discipline which will stand you in good stead in all sorts of circumstances.

It may seem helpful to talk to others about the way you have been hurt but in the long run it does more damage and increases bad feeling. Proverbs gives priceless advice when it says 'He who covers over an offence promotes love, but whoever repeats the matter separates close friends' (Proverbs 17:9).

Strictly confidential?

'Now, I'm telling you this in the strictest of confidence'. Those words can spell danger because you may have been told something that needs to be passed on because of the way that it affects another person or because it has made you aware of something that is illegal. No-one can bind you to strict confidence and you have the right to use your own discretion. If a young person or child tells you that they are being abused you will need to check to see what the law of your country requires of you in such circumstances. This will involve agonising choices and will undoubtedly affect your relationship with the person who has confided in you but you must do what is right and in the best long term interests of everyone involved. There are four questions you should ask yourself.

- Does it affect another person and if so what will happen to him or her if I do not pass the information on?

- Is there something illegal involved?

- Will keeping this to myself harm people?

- Will passing this information on do harm?

If you decide to speak to someone affected by what you have been told or if you report it to the relevant authorities you may lose some friends – at least in the short term. But if you keep this to yourself you run the risk of seeing the situation escalate and may find yourself in deep trouble because you have not acted on it. In the short term this is a lose-lose situation, but in the long term, if you do the right thing, you will be pleasing God and maintaining your integrity.

Relationships can take the most surprising turns – especially in churches. But with the help of the Holy Spirit and careful application of Biblical principles, the majority of these problems can be overcome. We hope that this chapter will equip you to tackle some of these issues with confidence.

Chapter Three

Hiccups at work

THE BOSS IS A BEAST

Many years ago we both worked at the same government office. Each lunch time we would eat together in the employees' restaurant. The food was fantastic but when the head Chef was in a bad mood everyone in the kitchen would feel the impact; the staff – and the customers – needed to dive for cover. Work can be difficult when the boss is a beast.

When your boss gets difficult you may find that you cannot do anything to please them, as someone once wryly said, 'Accomplishing the impossible only means that the boss will add it to your regular duties.'

Alongside this there are the days when the boss is in a bad mood, resulting in unreasonable deadlines and the expectation that you should be chained to your desk until a task is finished irrespective of your home commitments.

There are two qualities essential in overcoming this problem: humility and patience. Humility makes you realise that you cannot handle this on your own and that you need God's help while patience will enable you to respond to your boss with grace that magnifies Christ. The meaning of the word translated as 'patience' or 'longsuffering' in the New Testament is 'the ability to endure injuries inflicted by others and the willingness to accept irritating or painful situations.'[2] Remember that if your colleagues know you are a Christian they will be watching your reaction very carefully. Make sure they see something different about you.

While it is important to act towards your difficult boss in a way that is consistent with your relationship with the Lord, not all practices are acceptable. If they make racist comments or subject the staff to a torrent of swear-words you are within your rights to ask them to stop and if they refuse to do so, to submit a complaint. There is nothing wrong with exercising your rights; Paul once saved himself from a public beating by claiming his rights as a Roman Citizen (see Acts 22:25). And if a boss is using any kind of sexual harassment or makes detrimental comments about the physical attributes of a member of staff it should be dealt with immediately.

Since God is in control of our lives everything that happens to us is in line with his purposes, you must accept that he has put you under the authority of this difficult person. Trust God to fulfil his plan and remember that ultimately you are working for the Lord and not the boss. The Bible tells us that 'there is no authority except that which God has established', (Rom 13:1) which means that God has put your manager over you and you must show respect whether they are good at their job or not.

THE BOSS IS A TURKEY

Gordon Brittas is one of our all time favourite comedy characters. He was the central character in the British TV programme, 'The Brittas Empire.' Brittas was the manager of a leisure centre and anything he touched seemed to turn to disaster. His people-skills were appalling, his ideas were off-the-wall and his day-to-day management of the centre was totally incompetent. Brittas' one saving grace was Laura, his deputy manager, who cleaned up after him and somehow managed to restore order.

If you are in the same position as Laura you may be very frustrated with your boss. You are the one who does all the work whilst he is the one who takes all the credit and a large proportion of you time seems to be spent sorting out mistakes he has made.

---

2. MacArthur Study Bible, comment on Galatians 5:22, Word, Nashville, 1997

Resist the human reaction to complain about him to your colleagues. Remember that the Bible tells you to 'do all things without grumbling or arguing' (Phil 2:14) and this is one of those 'all things'. However incompetent he or she is you must maintain respect for them so that you can do your job in a way that pleases the Lord.

INCOMPETENT COLLEAGUES

It is Friday morning, there is a pile of work to get through and you have braced yourself to dive into it. The first task has already been struck off your list and you are encouraged that if you keep up the momentum you will have the pile cleared by the end of the day. Then you become aware of your colleague standing by your desk: 'sorry to bother you,' she says, looking very flustered, 'but I think I've just lost this months sales data; what do you think I should do?' You both know that if you speak to the manager about it he or she will hit the roof so you decide to help her. By eleven-thirty you have sorted it out but you lose all hope of achieving the goals you set yourself at the beginning of the morning.

An incompetent colleague can be a huge drain on your time and your patience. They may be more likely to gravitate to you because, as a Christian, you will treat them kindly. However, if this problem is not addressed your own work may suffer.

Make sure that you always show patience and kindness in the way you deal with them; as well as being the right thing to do this will also be a great witness to them. However, your first responsibility is to get your own work done and if they are your equal, rather than your subordinate, you should not feel that it is your responsibility to carry them. Sometimes you will need to be firm and say 'I can spare five minutes but after that I must get back to my own work' and you should never feel that you have to cover for them; they must take responsibility for themselves. You could offer to spend a lunchtime helping them to understand how to do the job better or stay behind after work but be careful to set limits. Sometimes as Christians we are taken advantage of and there is little or no merit in this.

CAUGHT IN THE CROSSFIRE

Once they were the best of friends but now Gladys and Jackie are sworn enemies. Some time ago they had a quarrel and they now cannot stand the sight of each other. The problem is that you work with them and become caught in the middle of their conflict. It is not easy when you find yourself caught in the crossfire especially if each of them asks you what the other person has said about them.

The most important quality you need to exercise is boldness. Both Jackie and Gladys need to be told that you are not interested in what they dislike about each other. You can put a positive emphasis on it and say that you like them both and would love it if you could all get along. This may initially draw their displeasure and scorn but in the long-run it will prevent you from being used as a pawn in their battle-of-wits against each other. Never let yourself get drawn into any of their arguments, if you do you will be the one who comes out the worst.

Make this a matter of prayer before you go to work and follow Nehemiah's example with a quiet, urgent request for God's help when you do not know how to respond to the feud.

Jesus said 'blessed are the peacemakers' (Matt 5:9) and this situation will give you the ability to put that into practice.

TOO CLOSE FOR COMFORT

If there was anything complicated or urgent to be done in the office it would be passed on to Jerry and Alice. They had been working together for the past two years and their complimentary skills made them a great team. Jerry was a Christian, and had on several occasions, spoken to Alice about his faith and she had attended some special services at his church. Having worked so closely they had got to know each other very well and discovered that they had similar tastes in music, so in the rare times when they were able to have a break, they had plenty to talk about. The most recent task they had been given was the most difficult yet and they were at their desks long after everyone else had gone home. When they eventually finished they decided to get something to eat. As usual their conversation was all about the latest CD's they had bought and new music each had discovered.

On the way home Jerry could not stop thinking about Alice and he became aware of feelings towards her. It seemed quite innocent; he did not lust after her or have unclean thoughts but felt just like he did when he had his first crush on a girl as a teenager. He told himself this could not be true. After all he and Alice had been working together for years and there had never been an inkling of anything between them before.

It all seemed a bit silly when he finally walked through the front door, hugged his wife and got swamped by his children. But the next morning, on the way to work, he felt excited at the thought of seeing Alice again and when he got into the office he did not know quite how to act towards her. In fact his behaviour was so out of character that she asked him if he was feeling unwell.

During the lunch-break Jerry took a walk in the park and realised that if he did not do something to stop this, he could be in spiritual and moral danger. His friend had developed a relationship with a female colleague, which led to the break-up of his marriage, and Jerry was determined not do the same thing. If he dealt with this now it would not develop into something dangerous.

Wrong relationships and affairs rarely, if ever, happen instantly; people take a series of steps towards them. Jerry realized this and was able to put a stop to it at the earliest possible stage. Sadly not everyone is so sensible. People often go into denial and convince themselves that there is nothing wrong with the relationship, justifying each step they take. You may assure yourself that you are only having lunch together but if it becomes a regular appointment you will inevitably become closer. If you tell someone that you have feelings for them you will be giving the impression that you want to take things further. And before long the relationship falls headlong into a sinful affair that will leave betrayal and destruction of families in its path. Since this is a book about small problems we will be concentrating on how to act as soon as those feelings begin.

Read the warning signs

Jerry's feelings towards Alice were the first warning sign that their relationship was in danger of developing into an affair. If you can identify with this, think back to the circumstances that led to the feelings.

- Have you had a conversation that has been a little more intimate than normal?
- Have you had any light physical contact?
- Did you give a lingering glance in his / her direction?
- Have your eyes met and you both held the gaze for an instant and then laughed it off?
- Have you been spending a little more time together than necessary?[3]

It is vital that you deal with the factors that have triggered these feelings and keep your contact to work-time only. Think about your body language, avoiding a light hand on the shoulder or looking into his or her eyes and making sure that you do not sit too closely to each other.

When people have romantic feelings for someone they will often have a rose-rimmed picture of them as the perfect person; the reality is always very different. The feelings you are experiencing now cast a golden glow over the other person which may leave your wife or husband looking very different. However, the person you are working with is on his or her best behaviour with you, she will have spent time carefully applying her make up and be dressed in designer clothes and he will be decked out in his new suit and covered in the aroma of an expensive aftershave. You are seeing each other at your most presentable when you see your spouse in all kinds of circumstances. A Christian University Professor once candidly said: 'I leave for work in the morning, the children are crying and my wife hasn't even had a chance to comb her hair. She looks tired from a sleepless night and she only has time to peck me on the cheek when I go out of the door. When I arrive at work my pretty research assistant smiles sweetly to me; that is where my feelings start to kick in.' The Professor went on to say that he dealt with it by

---

3. I am grateful to 'The Snare' by Lois Mowday's Navpress 1988, for the formulation of these questions.

realising that those feelings were based on a comparison that he should not be making. If you are comparing your spouse to a colleague (or anyone else) the warning lights should be flashing furiously. Tell yourself that this is completely false and refuse to entertain such thoughts. Instead think about the great qualities your wife or husband has.

Talk about your husband or wife

If you talk about your spouse you will be sending out a message that says you are committed to your marriage. Have their picture on your desk and if possible invite your colleague to your home so that they can meet your spouse. If your colleague is married ask about their husband or wife and never get involved in a discussion about any problems there may be in their marriage.

Filter out flirting

Flirting is often seen as harmless fun but in reality it is a very dangerous practice. We have known many instances where it has led to immoral relationships. Do not entertain it and never deceive yourself into thinking that it is innocent. Ask the Lord to examine the way you behave towards people of the opposite sex and consider whether you would be acting in the same way if your wife or husband were with you.

AM I IN THE RIGHT JOB?

Ever since, as a boy he had watched Perry Mason, Nathan wanted to be a lawyer. He was not attracted by the money or the prestige, but the ability to help people get justice. It was not an easy career path to choose and involved sacrificing a lot of personal time when he could have been out enjoying himself with his friends. Nathan read law at university and passed with a good degree before going to law school where he also did well.

It was in the first few months as a junior employee of a big law firm specialising in commercial law, that Nathan began to have nagging doubts as to whether he was following the right career. The profit-driven environment of corporate law seemed a world away from the dedicated professionalism shown by Perry Mason. However, he brushed the doubts aside and worked hard. He soon became an established employee and the Partners trusted him with more complex and demanding cases, but the more successful he became, the less satisfied he was with his chosen career. He had dreamed of doing this job, worked hard to get to his present position but now he wondered if he was doing the right thing at all.

If you find your work satisfying you can live with most of the difficulties it throws at you but if you wake up on Monday morning thinking 'what am I doing this for?' Work can become a source of immense frustration. You will probably have phases in ways you regard your work; at times it may be stimulating while on other occasions it may seem disappointing or frustrating. But if you are constantly dissatisfied with it, you would be right to ask yourself whether you are in the right job.

Guidance can be a complex and confusing subject and at a time like this you may be asking the Lord to show you whether you are in the right place. It becomes a lot simpler when you realise that God has given you a mind and rather than expecting a sign to fall out of the sky you can apply some Biblical principles and prayerfully think them through.

Principle #1: Commitment to Christ

Jesus never sought converts – only disciples and he said that anyone who wants to follow him must 'take up his cross daily' (Luke 9:23). Now that the sacrificial system is finished you only need to make one offering – yourself. In Romans we are commanded to be a 'living sacrifice holy and acceptable to God' (Rom 12.1) which means that the whole of our lives must be consumed by a dedication to Christ.

Principle #2: Holiness

Everyone who is committed to Christ wants to know God's will for their life. Whilst the Bible does not tell you who you should marry (except that it should be another Christian) and what job you should be doing, it does declare that it is God's will for you to be holy. That simply means that you should be separate and distinct. When Paul wrote to the Christians in Thessalonica about this he said:

> 'It is God's will that you should be sanctified: that you should avoid sexual immorality; that each of you should learn to control his own body in a way that is holy and honourable, not in passionate lust like the heathen, who do not know God' (1 Thessalonians 4:3-5).

Principle #3: God has given us a new perspective

Before you became a Christian your sights were set on everything this world had to offer but now you are 'a citizen of heaven' (Phil 3:20). Success and prosperity may have been at the top of your agenda before you knew Christ but now your greatest aim should be to hear him greet you with the words 'well done good and faithful servant' when you cross the threshold of heaven.

Principle #4: You have a responsibility to your family

The Bible commands you to take your responsibility to care for your family very seriously (1 Timothy 5:8). You should not launch out into a situation without considering their needs and gaining the support of your spouse.

Principle #5: God calls his children to honest hard-work

Some of the young Christians in Thessalonica had become so excited about the prospect of the Lord's return that they had downed tools and stopped working in expectation of the great event. This caused tension with other believers so Paul wrote to them saying:

> 'Make it your ambition to lead a quiet life, to mind your own business and to work with your hands, just as we told you, so that

your daily life may win the respect of outsiders and so that you will not be dependent on anybody' (1 Thessalonians 4:11-12).

There is nothing 'spiritual' about leaving your job with nothing else to go onto. Even though you may have the money to support yourself for a period of time if you are below retirement age you should be working or training for a new vocation.

Within these constraints you have the freedom to choose what job you should be doing. The important thing is not whether you should be a refuse-collector, a postman or a lawyer but that you are totally committed to Christ, living a holy life and providing for your family by doing honest work.

After a lot of thought and prayer Nathan decided to leave the law firm and re-train to be a teacher. The work was a big challenge to him but he felt as if his gifts and abilities were being put to good use and since starting his most recent post he has been able to launch a Christian Fellowship in the school.

PASSED OVER FOR PROMOTION – AGAIN!

The date that has been ringed on the calendar for weeks has now finally arrived. Today you will find out whether you have got the promotion you have been working hard for. You enter the office, sit at your desk and get down to work but every time the boss walks by your desk your stomach flutters. Around mid-morning he starts to call people into his office. Some come out looking elated while others look despondent. Eventually it is your turn and you can immediately tell by his expression that it not going to be good news. He makes a joke to lighten the atmosphere (which is not very funny) and shuffles some papers on his desk, 'Gill, I'm so sorry; you did not get the promotion.' He gives you a few minutes to process the information and tries to sound more upbeat about it, 'never mind, it is not the end of the matter. You are a very valuable employee and personally I'd hate to lose you. Maybe you'll be successful next year!' You try to contain yourself and force a smile and say 'yes Mr. Grimshaw, thank you for letting me know.' The most upsetting part is that those you think deserved it least seemed to have been promoted because they were the boss' favourite while you worked hard and got another rejection.

You are right to be angry about this but it is important that you handle it in a way that honours the Lord. Some of the Psalmists expressed their fury and frustration to God without censure from him (see Psalm 69 and 109). As soon as you possibly can, get alone with God and pour out your heart to him. He knows everything about you and will completely understand your sense of injustice and your disappointment. Ask God to search your heart (see Psalm 139:22-23) and to show you if you are harbouring bitterness or jealousy and thank him that your 'times are in his hands' (Psalm 31:15).

When you get back to your desk you may think 'what is the use of working hard anyway?' This is an understandable reaction but the Bible tells us to do our work for the Lord, not for people. Although you have been treated unfairly you can accept this with grace by doing your day-to-day tasks for him: 'Whatever you do, work at it with all your heart, as working for the Lord, not for men' (Colossians 3:23). The workplace will probably be awash with gossip about the promotions and others who have been passed over may try to draw you into a negative discussion about those who have succeeded. Do your best to avoid this; you can be certain that it will not benefit you.

Paul said 'if it was only in this life that we hoped we would be men to be most pitied' (1 Cor 15:19). When you think about this disappointment in the light of eternity it will seem very different. You may have lost out on a challenging job and some extra cash but other than that it will have no bearing on the things that really matter.

THE NEVER ENDING STORY

Despite having faster computers and efficient technology people seem to be working harder than ever today. Sometimes life seems to consist only of work and sleep with a little time for eating slotted in (if you can spare it!). If you have come to the point where you realise that something has to be done about it, here are some simple steps.

- Establish your priorities

Take a couple of sheets of paper. On one write what is essential to you: living for the Lord, caring for your family, working efficiently and serving the Lord in your church. Then on the other sheet write down what else is consuming your time. Is there anything at work or in church you can delegate? Is there something you need to give up?

- Set boundaries

At some point in time the boundaries between work and your family life may have been broken down. This is often a result of gradual erosion and it will take a concerted effort to establish them. However, for the sake of your sanity you may need to decide where to draw the line and to communicate this to your employer. If you are running your own business it may be necessary to think about hiring extra help so that you can block off time to be with your family, to rest and to serve the Lord in your local church. Remember the old saying: 'you will never get to the end of your life and say "I wish I'd spent more time in the office."'

- Keep your spouse informed

When you are surrounded by work it is easy to get so immersed in what you are doing that you forget to tell your nearest and dearest that you have been delayed. Make it a discipline to tell your wife or husband if you will be late home.

- Don't just soldier on

Christians often accept the realities of overwork and battle on without complaint. Whilst we would not want to encourage discontent or grumbling there is nothing wrong in telling your employer that you are struggling to keep up. You never know what the result may be.

A balancing act

Have you ever watched someone juggle balls in the air? It can look deceptively simple but it is a very difficult art to master. There will be many people reading this book who are desperately trying to juggle the demands made upon their time from work, family and church. There is no easy solution to this increasingly growing problem but we can point you in the right direction towards solving these tensions in your life.

Some important questions

You will need to set a little time in your schedule aside to ask yourself some important questions.

- What are my priorities?
- Am I meeting them?
- What do I need to change in order to do so?

Modern life is so demanding and complex you will be unlikely to find a permanent solution to the problem of balancing your priorities; this is something to be re-evaluated on a weekly basis. One week there may be extra family commitments such as parent's evenings or a school concert while another week there might be important things going on in your church that you will need to give extra attention to. Make sure that you are flexible with your programme, realistic about what you are able to do and clear about your priorities.

Some warnings

There are three dangers you can fall into when trying to balance time between work, family and church.

1. The danger of work becoming a god so that it rules your life.

Many people get so absorbed in their job that it is more important than anything else in their life. They may not readily admit this but it is has actually become more important to them than God and has therefore turned into an idol.

2. The danger of neglecting your family.

You can become so engrossed with your job and church activities that you become a stranger to your family. This will inevitably lead to tensions and difficulties.

3. The danger of making your family an idol.

Sometimes Christians can swing to the opposite extreme and put their family before the Lord so that everything they do centres around their family rather than God. Be careful that it does not take such an important place in your life that you 'neglect the assembling of yourselves together' (Heb 10:25). If you want the best for your family you must set an example in the way that you put God first and help them to walk in his ways.

Couples without families

Couples without children also struggle with balancing work, church and time together, and they are more prone to get things out of kilter because they do not have demands that a family make on them. If you are in this position you must ensure that you have quality time together. Meet one another for lunch, go out for dinner or spend a Saturday out in the country.

From the day that Adam and Eve took a bite from the forbidden fruit and unleashed the power of sin into the world, work has been infused with problems, heartache and toil. Each day you leave the house and take the journey to the factory or the office you can be confident that there will be a whole host of challenges awaiting you. As Christians we know that the curse has been undone and look forward to the time when all of these difficulties will be no more. In the meantime we can tackle them with the hope of what is to come and in the power of the Holy Spirit.

Chapter Four
Hiccups in the Christian life

SPIRITUAL PROBLEMS

BIBLE READING BLUES

At first you could not get enough of God's Word: the teaching of Jesus and the amazing miracles he performed, the great men and women of the Old Testament such as Gideon, Moses and Joshua and the New Testament Letters that gave you tremendous practical help with your Christian life. You may not be able to pinpoint when it happened, but over a period of time the Bible began to seem a bit dry to you. Now you are trying to plough through a list of names in Chronicles and reading God's Word has become a chore instead of joy.

This is a problem that many people are embarrassed to talk about. After all, the Bible is 'a lamp to [our] feet' (Psalm 119:105), it is inspired – literally 'breathed out' – by God (2 Tim 3:16). To admit that you are finding it hard to read sounds as if you are denying the fact that God has spoken and continues to speak through it. Of course one thing we should establish is that the fault never lies with God's Word: it is his revelation and has no error. The problem will lie with you, but you are not alone because at times all Christians go through a phase when they find reading the Bible a labour. The most common reasons are that people get stuck into a rut and lose the freshness they once had when spending time in God's Word. Here are some ways to regain the initiative so that the Bible becomes an inspiration again.

Stand back and look at the big picture

When visiting art galleries you may notice that some people stand back from the paintings to view them from a distance. This helps them see how all the details come together to form the big picture. The same principle needs to be applied to the way we read the Bible. It is a collection of sixty-six books, with different kinds of literature such as history, poetry, prophecy and letters and yet it has one unifying theme – to reveal God's plan in Christ. That may sound a bit of a challenge to grasp but it is not as difficult as you may think. Christ is the key to understanding God's plan; he is the centre and apex of it. So whenever you are reading the Bible ask yourself how the passage you are in it points to Christ and how he fulfils it. If you are reading about the offerings and sacrifices you will realise they have been fulfilled in Jesus' death on the cross. Gideon's defeat of the Midianites reminds us that Christ has defeated the powers of death and darkness: every victory in the Old Testament is an anticipation of the great victory that Christ has won.

God's promise to Abraham lies at the other end of the time-line.

> The Lord said to Abram, "Leave your country, your people and your father's household and go to the land I will show you. I will make you into a great nation and I will bless you; I will make your name great, and you will be a blessing.' (Genesis 12:1-2).

Dale Ralph Davis says that this promise concerns people, protection, presence, programme and place. If you read the events that unfold in the Old Testament in the light of this promise you will be able to understand more of the way in which God was working out his purposes.[4]

---

4. See Davis, Dale Ralph, 'The Word became Fresh', Christian Focus Publications, Tain, 2006, page 32-32

Since this is a book about small problems we cannot go into this in great detail but we recommend Vaughn Roberts book 'The Big Picture'. Once you see a passage as part of God's overarching revelation you will have a better appreciation of the way in which God works out his purpose and a fresh excitement about discovering this for yourself as you read his Word.

Don't get bogged down in detail

If you have sat through Bible studies about the significance of the tent pegs in the tabernacle or analysed the sacrifices and offerings in intricate detail you will probably not remember them as the most stimulating times you have ever had. You may have used a similar pattern yourself: carefully checking through a list of names or meticulously examining every aspect about the burnt offerings. Some Christians do the same with end-time prophecy and spend so long speculating the identity of 'the beast' that they read little else of God's Word. We would encourage you to avoid this. If you find yourself reading through a list of names in Chronicles, or the details of how the material for Solomon's Temple was gathered in 2 Kings, read through at a fairly brisk pace and keep in mind how they accomplish the promise given to Abraham in Genesis 12:1-2 and how they are fulfilled in Christ. Genealogies are important in that they trace a family line, which often has David as the centre-point and should be understood in the light of Jesus' genealogies in the Gospels.

Talk to a friend

You may assume that you are the only person who has ever struggled in this area. This is something which our enemy — 'the accuser' (Rev 12:10) — will play on. However, if you share this with a friend you will undoubtedly find that at some point he or she has faced the same problem and will be able to tell you how they came through it. They may even be struggling with it now; in which case you can work at it together.

Use a different translation

It is good to find a translation you are comfortable with and stick to it. However sometimes the occasional use of one that you are not quite so familiar with can bring a new freshness to what you are reading.

Do something different

While Simon recommends systematic reading of the Bible he always adds that you should feel free to break from it to do something different from time to time. It may be that you are stuck in a rut and need to take another approach for a little while. You could follow a character study, look at a theme or use some Bible notes. The Bible reading plan provided in Simon's book 'Improving your Quiet Time' is undated so that you can return to it without having to spend time catching up. The book also provides a whole range of different kinds of devotions to use in your Quiet Times. [5]

DRY PATCHES

The first time you hit a dry patch you will not know what is happening to you. Your zeal seems to have zeroed out, praying is hard and worship services become events you endure rather than enjoy. To prepare for this keep the following facts at the forefront of your mind.

 # Fact one: Dry patches are a normal part of the Christian life

After Jesus was baptised and the Holy Spirit came upon him in the form of a dove we are told that he 'was led by the Spirit in the desert' (Luke 4:1). There may be times in your life when the Holy Spirit leads you into a spiritual desert; there is nothing abnormal or wrong about you, it is part of God's plan for your life.

 # Fact two: Dry patches are one of God's tools

God knows everything about you (see Psalm 139) and he understands what is best for your growth as a Christian. If your life was one long blessing you

5. See Robinson, Simon, 'Improving your Quiet Times', Day One Publications, Leominster, 2005

would probably get intoxicated with the euphoria of the experience and take your eyes away from the Lord. But if your Christian life was a constant grind you would find it very hard to keep going. That is why he takes you through cycles: there will be times of great joy and blessing but they may be followed by difficulty and trial. God will use your dry patches to draw you closer and to teach you to depend on him. Memorise the following verse; you will find it very precious when you are in the middle of a dry period:

> 'Therefore I am now going to allure her; I will lead her into the desert and speak tenderly to her' (Hosea 2:14).

Look for God's tender hand on your life and pray that you will not waste this opportunity to get closer to him.

Fact three: It will not last forever

Have you ever spent a long period of time in an airport between flights? After a while it seems as if you have never been anywhere else. You may have a similar experience during a time of spiritual dryness when it has gone on for such a long time that seems as if it is never going to end. However that is not true; you will emerge from this difficult period and will be a stronger Christian for it.

With those facts in mind what should you do to navigate the wilderness when you find yourself there?

- **Keep going**

Do not give up your quiet times and do not tail off from attending church and getting together with other Christians – keep on. This will be the test of your commitment to Christ and his Kingdom. Are you going to follow him only when things are good or through all kinds of conditions? Memorise these verses and use them as a basis for some of your prayer times.

> 'But one thing I do: Forgetting what is behind and straining towards what is ahead, I press on towards the goal to win the

prize for which God has called me heavenwards in Christ Jesus.'
(Philippians 3:13-14)

- Depend on the Lord

The power to live the Christian life is not found in human effort but in divine strength. Paul refused to boast about his strengths and told people about his weaknesses:

> 'That is why, for Christ's sake, I delight in weaknesses, in insults, in hardships, in persecutions, in difficulties. For when I am weak, then I am strong' (2 Corinthians 12:10).

This will be a time during which you will become painfully aware of your weakness, but it will give you the opportunity to depend on God's power rather than your own strength.

- Go for growth

See this dry patch as God's boot camp in which he will train and develop you.

- Pray persistently

This is the most obvious thing to do but it can easily become neglected; especially as it can be difficult to pray during a dry patch. Here is a prayer from the Bible that you can use during such times:

> O God, you are my God,
> earnestly I seek you;
> my soul thirsts for you,
> my body longs for you,
> in a dry and weary land

where there is no water.
I have seen you in the sanctuary
and beheld your power and your glory.
Because your love is better than life,
my lips will glorify you.
I will praise you as long as I live,
and in your name I will lift up my hands.
My soul will be satisfied as with the richest of foods;
with singing lips my mouth will praise you.
On my bed I remember you;
I think of you through the watches of the night.
Because you are my help,
I sing in the shadow of your wings.
My soul clings to you;
your right hand upholds me.
(Psalm 63:1-8)

IT'S HARD TO PRAY

Justin was the most vocal member of the youth group: if there was a prayer-
time he would always be the first to contribute and if the Pastor asked people
to come forward to talk about what God had done in their lives he was out
like a shot. Initially Julia was impressed and encouraged by the way he
described his prayer life. According to Justin he prayed for thirty minutes
every morning and the same amount of time in the evening. She tried it for
herself but it did not seem to work. The first five minutes went well, the next
five dragged a little and the rest of the time her mind wandered and she
decided that there was no point in praying if she could not do it as well as
Justin.

In reality Justin struggled with praying as much as anyone else but his
ability to be able to talk for long periods of time probably seeped into his
prayer life. Most people however, probably identify with Julia and can find
prayer difficult both publicly and privately.

Praying publicly

Justin's prayers are a torrent of Bible verses related to a specific theme. He prays with insight, fervour and confidence. Julia, on the other hand, gets a bit lost for words. She has made some attempts during the prayer meeting but feels as if her prayers peter out halfway through. If you can identify with her, do not be intimidated by people who pray like Justin; just be yourself and say a simple prayer. Remember 'man looks at the outward but God looks at the heart' (1 Sam 16:7).

Although you are praying publicly you are addressing God rather than the other people in the room, so do not worry about what they are thinking. If you think your nerves may get the better of you and you could forget what to pray about, jot down a few bullet points on a piece of paper to prompt you.

Praying privately

When you get alone to pray do not try to be like someone else who has impressed you - be yourself. Your Heavenly Father knows everything about you and he will not be taken in by an act that you put on before him.

A journal is an invaluable way to keep a record of the things you have been praying about and to write down prayer points. Sometimes a change of environment can help too: Simon often goes out to the countryside to spend time in prayer.

Use the Bible to help you — it is full of prayers. Paul opens many of his letters by praying for the Christians he writes to (see Phil 1:1-11, Eph 1:15-23, 1 Thess 1:2-3) and many Psalms are the prayers of anguished men (see Psalms 12, 35 and 54). In addition there are the great prayers of Jesus' prayer (John 17), Nehemiah (Neh 2), and Daniel (Daniel 9). Jesus has also given us a great template in the prayer that he taught his disciples (see Matt 5:9-13).

MY CHURCH IS DEAD

You ask your friends about the church they belong to and their faces light up as they excitedly tell you everything that God is doing there. The question you dread is: 'and how about yours?' Should you put on a brave face, think hard and tell them about the few encouraging things or should you pour out your feelings of doom and gloom?

In these days Christians can be fickle and go wherever the biggest crowds and best music can be found. It is good that there are still people like you who commit themselves to a church because it is faithful to the gospel and in their locality. But it can have its problems when your friends talk endlessly about the strengths of the lively fellowship they belong to while you struggle.

Look for the good things

Instead of focusing on what you do not like about your church identify the things that are great about it. It may be the teaching or the relationships, or the children's work but you will find that once you begin, the list will keep growing. Hazel's mum used to quote the words of an old song:

> 'You've got to accentuate the positive,
>   eliminate the negative
>   and don't mess with Mr. In-between!'

Are you part of the solution?

Think of positive steps you can take which will help to change your church. Have you ever offered to play your instrument in the services or do a children's talk? Is there a practical task you can do for the Pastor to free him up to concentrate on other areas of the church's life? Ask yourself whether you are perpetuating the problem or contributing to the solution.

Be an encourager

The New Testament tells us that when we meet together we should 'encourage one another—and all the more as [we] see the Day approaching' (Hebrews 10:25). Sadly, if a church is struggling, most people talk about what they do not like and this can make things worse. You can break the pattern by encouraging people to go on in their relationship with God, to support the church leaders and to pray about the situation. Encourage the church leaders and tell them that you are praying for them – it will make a lot of difference to their work.

When Christians from the same church get talking, the conversation can easily slip into a negative mode; if this happens to you, stop the discussion in its tracks, seize on something positive and spend a few moments in prayer with the people concerned.

EVERYONE'S SO SPIRITUAL!

Ivan gave Pete a friendly thump on the back. 'Hi brother, how are you doing, are you still praising God and have you seen any great miracles in your life recently?' Pete could not think of anything to report. 'Not really Ivan, how about you?' Ivan's huge grin seemed to meet each of his ears, 'Well bro, have you got a few hours?' And for the next ten minutes (thankfully not the hours that had been promised) Pete was given a list of triumphs and miracles that seemed to be a daily occurrence in Ivan's life. He nodded and smiled but all along he was desperate to get away from Ivan, wondering whether the problem was that he was not as spiritual as him.

Jane had been a Christian since she was a child. She was committed to the Lord and disciplined in her quiet times but her Christian friends seemed to be a lot more serious than she was. They kept to their own group in school (known as the 'holy Jo's'), and only listened to Gospel music. Jane on the other hand mixed with everyone and had a wide taste in music. When she told her Christian friends that she found a lot of Christian music 'cheesy' they reacted as if she had said that she did not believe in the Virgin Birth! She liked these girls but after spending time with them she always went away feeling like she was a second-rate Christian.

There are times when other Christians can make you feel this way and cause you to have doubts about the quality of your walk with the Lord. If you are in this position here are some principles to help get things into perspective.

No-one should judge you

Paul had a similar problem with some people at Corinth who considered him unimpressive and simple. This was his response:

> 'I care very little if I am judged by you or by any human court; indeed, I do not even judge myself. My conscience is clear, but that does not make me innocent. It is the Lord who judges me. Therefore judge nothing before the appointed time; wait till the Lord comes. He will bring to light what is hidden in darkness and will expose the motives of men's hearts. At that time each will receive his praise from God' (1 Corinthians 4:3-5).

People have no right to judge you by the standards they have set. Ask the Lord to show you anything you need to put right in your own life; he knows everything about you but they do not.

Be yourself

Their behaviour is actually a subtle form of peer pressure but instead of pressuring you to act badly they are trying to force you into the mould of Christianity they have made for themselves. Do not try to be anyone other than yourself.

It is the long haul that matters

Our experience of people like Ivan is that although they begin with a flurry of activity they often burn out very quickly. We have found that it is those who make steady progress who carry on and get to the finishing line.

PERSONAL PROBLEMS

TEMPER, TEMPER

It starts out as an exchange of different points of view but quickly develops into a heated argument and before you know it you are the one who explodes in a fit of temper and storms off. Twenty minutes later you have simmered down and feel completely ashamed of yourself. It does not happen very often but you wish it never did.

If you suffer from occasional but significant outbursts of temper here are some facts to face up to.

Fact One: Self-control is a fruit of the Spirit

Ask someone to cite the fruit of the Spirit and you can guarantee they will come up with love, joy and peace but they may not get as far as self-control. However it is a mark of the Holy Spirit at work within you and will be displayed in your life when you shun the way of the flesh and 'keep in step with the Spirit' (Gal 5:25). You will do this by restraining yourself when your emotions and passions push you towards losing your temper and depending on God's Spirit to live out the new life you have been given in Christ.

Fact Two: You have a new nature

Ralph was a difficult man. During church business meetings he would rise to his feet, correcting the grammar of the minutes and aggressively reminding the chairman of points of order. In conversation he could be rude and cutting and if he lost his temper (usually about something very trivial) everyone in the church knew about it. One Sunday he stormed up to the church Secretary and shouted, in a deliberately slow and precise manner: 'where are my minutes?' Chrissie had not long moved to the area and was new to the church. When she witnessed one of Ralph's outbursts she was utterly shocked. 'Does he always act that way?' she asked her friend (who had known him for twenty years). 'Ah, don't worry, that's just Ralph's manner, he can't help being a grump - he was born that way!' Chrissie was not satisfied with the answer she had been given stating 'well, he may have been born like that but he was not born again like it!'

Chrissie had got right to the heart of the issue: Ralph may have had a tendency for outbursts of temper in his old nature but it did not belong to his new life. The Bible calls us to 'put on the new self, which is being renewed in knowledge in the image of its Creator' (Col 3:10). You may claim to have inherited your quick temper from your father, mother or even a grandparent but it is part of your old nature which you must 'put off' in preference to the new.

> 'Put to death, therefore, whatever belongs to your earthly nature: sexual immorality, impurity, lust, evil desires and greed, which is idolatry. Because of these, the wrath of God is coming. You used to walk in these ways, in the life you once lived. But now you must rid yourselves of all such things as these: anger, rage, malice, slander and filthy language from your lips. Do not lie to each other, since you have taken off your old self with its practices and have put on the new self, which is being renewed in knowledge in the image of its Creator' (Colossians 3:5-10).

Fact Three: Outbursts of temper can only do harm

Once the adrenaline has worn off you will regret many of the things that have been said and will need to repair the damage that has been done. This will involve asking for God's forgiveness and apologising to the person who has been at the receiving end of angry words. Remember James' warning: 'man's anger does not bring about the righteous life that God desires' (James 1:20).

Here are some ways you can control your temper when you find it welling up.

- Stop while you can

Proverbs says that 'Starting a quarrel is like breaching a dam; so drop the matter before a dispute breaks out' (Proverbs 17:14). It is better to keep quiet and walk away while you are on good terms with someone than to get drawn into an argument that runs the risk of getting out of control.

- Never get personal

You can tell that an argument is becoming out of hand when you start making personal remarks about the other person. As soon as you find yourself doing so, stop and apologise suggesting that you find a more relaxed way to discuss the differences you have.

- Keep control

Proverbs – which is one of the most helpful books of the Bible to read on this subject - says that 'a man who lacks self-control is like a city whose walls are broken down' (Prov 25:28). As soon as you sense those 'walls' beginning to crack ask your Heavenly Father to enable you to exercise self control. See it as an opportunity in which you can grow as a Christian.

- Get a sense of perspective

If you look back over the things you have lost your temper over it is unlikely that many of them have any lasting significance. Ask yourself if the issue is really important enough to risk polluting yourself with an outburst of temper and alienating the person you are talking to.

LOVING SOMEONE YOU DON'T LIKE

Chris was a very popular leader at youth camps because of his easy-going nature. He got on with just about everyone; he was rarely annoyed and let people work at their own pace. As the number of young people attending the camp grew, Chris found himself more stretched, so the Board decided to help him by appointing Sam as a co-leader to help shoulder the responsibility. At first Chris was delighted about this but after a few days he became aware of a big personality difference existing between them. Sam liked everything to run to a time-table and felt the need to be in control and to be kept constantly informed of what was going on. Being a stickler for rules and regulations he handed Chris a list of jobs that needed to be done to bring things up to 'a decent standard'. It was not long before tensions began to emerge. Chris struggled with his relationship with Sam, he was not bitter or unloving but he found it difficult to like Sam because the two of them were so different.

Many people confuse liking someone with loving them. The Bible commands us to love one another; Jesus said that this would enable people to recognise that we are his disciples (John 13.34). To love someone is to accept them as they are and treat them with kindness and patience (see 1 Cor 13) but to like them is to appreciate characteristics in them that you find endearing. If you find yourself in the same position as Chris you do not need to feel obliged to like them but you must put the qualities given in 1 Cor 13 into practice and love them. Love, in the New Testament, is undeserving: you do not demonstrate it because of what a person is like or what they have done. The greatest example of this is the love that God showed to us in that 'while we were still sinners Christ died for us' (Rom 5:8). The real test of your capacity to love people is when you have to spend time with someone you would not naturally be drawn to. However, you do not have to do it in your own strength: love is a fruit of the Spirit.

The danger of disliking someone is that it may go beyond the things that grate on you and grow into bitterness. It is no wonder that Hebrews tells us to be sure that 'no bitter root grows up to cause trouble and defile many' (Heb 12:15). If you become bitter and resentful towards someone, it may not be long before you let other people know your feelings, which will bring about disunity and increase tension. So while not liking someone is a small hiccup, if not handled properly it can develop into a full-scale problem.

To help get things into perspective, isolate the things you do not like about the person and then focus on the positive aspects of their character. In Chris' case he disliked the way Sam tried to control everything and order him about, but after giving it some thought he realised that there were many good qualities which he had not seen before. Sam was always thoughtful and considerate and never spoke badly about anyone. This helped Chris to see him in a new light and get on with him better. Chris also decided to ask Sam to spend some time with him in a relaxed atmosphere to ease things between them and clear up their differences. They went to a local café and Chris stressed his desire for them to get on: 'I realise that we are very different,' he said, 'so I want to make sure there is no scope for misunderstanding or division between us.' Chris went on to tell Sam that, after running the camp for the last few years, he found it a little difficult to be organised. 'I am probably taking you the wrong way,' he added, 'So I wanted to clear things up between us.' Sam responded positively and explained that his 'controlling' tendencies arose from his anxieties about potential problems that may arise if things were not done in a particular way. After a good-natured discussion they left the café having set some ground rules about how they should treat one-another and clear up any misunderstandings. They went on to lead more camps together and realised they actually complimented one another!

Rather than get irritated about the way someone grates on you, thank God for your differences; after all, we cannot all be the same. Our differences can actually compliment one another.

You are not obliged to like someone but if you stick at it and celebrate, rather than despise your dissimilarities, like Chris you may be pleasantly surprised at what happens.

LITTLE TEMPTATIONS

Think of temptation and the image of Potiphar's wife trying to lure Joseph into adultery or a Director being attracted by the idea of embezzling the Company's money may come to mind. Little temptations – such as being jealous of another's success or wealth, a lustful glance, using a few sharp words, or laughing at a dirty joke can slip under the radar. However these things have the capability to inflict a lot of damage on you and on those around and they must be taken seriously.

The Babylonian government had implemented a programme to cream off the brightest and most promising young Jewish men so that their talents could be used in the expanding empire. Three young men had been uprooted from their homeland and taken to work in the Royal Palace and were welcomed with a huge banquet.

They were treated well and given food 'from the King's table'. If they had come from any other nation they would have revelled in the honour but these men were troubled about eating such food and politely refused. The book of Daniel does not tell us why they did this but it is safe to assume that they were concerned that by doing so they would break the laws God had given their people concerning what they should eat and drink. Despite his initial objections the Chief Official agreed to let them have a diet of bread and water for ten days and then review it. After the time had elapsed 'they looked healthier and more nourished than any of the young men who ate the royal food' (Dan 1:15). Because these young men dealt with the small temptations they were equipped to deal with the greater ones that lay ahead. Later on in the book of Daniel we are told that they faced an ultimatum to worship a statue of the King or lose their lives for refusing to. They could have given in and worshipped the image in order to preserve themselves but because they had already faced up to the smaller test they were able to stand up to the big one (see Daniel 3).

It is important to withstand small temptations in order to be prepared for bigger tests in the future. And the principles for dealing with them are the same as those for dealing with the bigger issues.

Be alert

Your enemy – Satan – knows your weaknesses and will exploit them to lure you into sin. Look out for ways in which he may try to exploit them to lure you from living for God. Vaughan Roberts suggests asking oneself the following question: 'If I were the devil, where would I direct the attack against myself to try to lead myself into sin?'[6]

Look for the escape route

The New Testament says that 'No temptation has seized you except what is common to man. And God is faithful; he will not let you be tempted beyond what you can bear. But when you are tempted, he will also provide a way out so that you can stand up under it' (1 Corinthians 10:13). Develop the art of looking for the escape route. In the Old Testament Joseph faced sexual temptation from his master's wife and he quickly found the most effective way to resist it – he ran away from her!

Learn from your failings

If you succumb to a small temptation do not wallow in a sense of defeat. Psalm 37 promises that when you fall you 'will not be hurled headlong, because the Lord is the One who holds [your] hand' (Psalm 37:24 NASB). He will pick you up and get you back on the right road. It would be constructive for you to spend a little time reflecting on what led you to fall in this way and to ask God to help you find a strategy to avoid letting it happen again.

DISCOURAGEMENT

After the heady atmosphere of his victory at Mount Carmel, Elijah came down to earth with a bump. He had faced down the Prophets of Baal and seen God at work dramatically. Then a short threatening message from evil Queen Jezebel – 'May the gods strike me and even kill me if by this time tomorrow I have not killed you just as you killed them'[7] –sent him fleeing for his life to Beersheba, the most southerly town in the Kingdom. When he arrived there he retreated to the desert and prayed: 'Take my life, for I am no better than my ancestors who have already died.'[8]

---

6. Vaughan, Battles Christians Face, Authentic Media, London, 2007, Page 137
7. 1 Kings 19.2, The New Living Translation
8. 1 Kings 19.4, The New Living Translation

A disappointment that had followed a monumental victory swept Elijah into discouragement. Many people can identify with him because it is often unexpected events and disappointments that knock us off course and lead to discouragement.

Robert had seen some great things happen in the college Christian Fellowship of which he was President: people had come to Christ, new programmes had been launched and everyone seemed in good spirits. A little dispute among a couple of members quickly developed into a full-scale argument that divided the fellowship. Despite the positive things that had happened he felt deflated and ready to give up.

Discouragement can be a powerful tool in Satan's hands so it is important to have a full armoury to deal with it.

Realism

When things are going well in Church or in the Christian life we would all like to think it will never end. In reality, whilst God blesses us with such periods he does not wrap us in cotton wool and allows difficult times to come into our lives. They will come in all shapes and sizes: disappointments, setbacks, opposition, conflict and unexpected circumstances but in some way or another they will arrive. Enjoy the good times while they last and gather your spiritual strength for the difficulties around the corner.

Perspective

One of the things we can observe from Elijah's experience of discouragement is that as soon as he hears the death-threat from Queen Jezebel he appears to forget the epic victory over the Prophets of Baal that God had given him. He had defeated hundreds of men who – given the chance - would have torn him to pieces and now he is laid low by the vitriolic words of one woman. Later on in the story he tells God that he is the only person 'who has not bowed the knee to Baal' but God puts it into perspective by telling him of one thousand people who have not swallowed the lie and worshipped this idol.

People who are laid low with discouragement often claim that they are the only ones committed to their area of Christian work or that they have been left on their own. If you are saying something similar, get a sense of perspective and look at the things God had been doing. Are you really on your own or are there others faithfully praying for you and supporting you?

Trust

Discouragement often arises when things do not turn out as you expect or when you have an unpleasant surprise. You may not know what is going on and where it will end but God is still in control. Talk to him about your uncertainties and frustrations and then rest in him.

Focus on solutions

One reason people get discouraged is that they become so wrapped up in their problems they cannot see a way out. The best antidote to this is to focus on possible solutions. Keep hold of the promise given in James 1:5: 'If any of you lacks wisdom, he should ask God, who gives generously to all without finding fault, and it will be given to him.'

Don't over-analyse

There is always a danger of 'analysis paralysis' - that is looking at a problem from every possible angle to try to see what is going on. This will only result in you using up a lot of much needed mental energy and getting you more entrenched in your discouragement. It is no surprise that Proverbs gives the exhortation to 'trust in the Lord with all your heart and lean not on your own understanding' (Prov 3:5-6). Only God knows the end from the beginning so it is best that you leave the problem in his hands and get on with living for him.

Talk about the positive things

It is a baffling fact that when Christians get together they often seem to spend a lot of time talking about negative things. This is about as helpful as switching on loud music when someone has a terrible headache. Talk about the things that have encouraged you, share your plans and dreams for the future and you will find that the cloud of discouragement hanging over you will quickly disburse.

GUILT

The Roman poet Nemo Malus Felix said 'Peace visits not the guilty mind'. When guilt directs a person to face up to their wrongdoing and to confess it to God it is productive. However it is usually a destructive force that gnaws away at the heart and mind. It is not always confined to big issues: you may spend the day eaten up with guilt about an unwise word you have said or a slip up you have made. If you find yourself in this position here are some questions to ask.

- Is my sense of guilt related to a sin?

If the answer is 'yes' confess the sin to God and get on with what he has given you to do. Remember the exhortation and promise given in the Bible: 'If we confess our sins, he is faithful and just and will forgive us our sins and purify us from all unrighteousness' (1 John 1:9).

- Is it about something I have already confessed?

Sometimes it takes time for our minds to catch up with God's promise and although you have asked God to forgive you, the sense of guilt may still remain. Remind yourself of the last part of that promise: 'he is faithful and just and will forgive us our sins and purify us from all unrighteousness.' Another helpful verse can be found in the Psalms: 'He has removed our sins from us as far as the east is from the west' (Psalm 103:12 New Living Translation).

- Do you feel condemned?

There is a world of difference between the way in which God shows us our sin and the way Satan goads us about it. The New Testament speaks of 'Godly sorrow [that] brings repentance'. If God is convicting you of sin he will forgive you and help you to get on with your Christian life but if you have a consistent sense of guilt and worthlessness you can be sure that Satan – 'the accuser' (Rev 21:10) – is behind it. In which case refuse to listen to his voice and thank God for the forgiveness you have through Christ. Remember that 'there is now no condemnation for those who are in Christ Jesus' (Romans 8:1).

- Is someone trying to make you feel guilty?

When you have wronged someone and asked for their forgiveness they can do one of two things: they can unconditionally forgive you (as God has forgiven us) or they can use the situation to exercise a sense of control over you. If they keep reminding you of the way you have hurt them they have not really forgiven and they are showing themselves to be manipulative. You have done what God has required of you and now you can move on without feeling that they have any hold over you.

WITNESSING WOES

The phone rang the second Sue walked in through the door laden with shopping. She frantically put her bags on the floor (bruising the fruit she had just bought) and grabbed the phone from its stand. There was a slight pause, a click and the telling sound of a murmur of different phone calls going on in the background. She did not recognise the voice of the person speaking to her 'Hello am I speaking to Susan Faversham?' Her suspicion came out in the tone of her answer 'Who wants to speak to her?' 'This is just a courtesy call from

Holiday Homes for You.' It had been a long day that had ended with an exasperating trip to the shops and this was the last straw for Sue: 'Look, I do not know where you got this number but you are not to ring me anymore!' She slammed the phone down and slumped into the armchair. Later on, after being revived by multiple cups of tea and a meal she went to her fellowship group and talked about her day and the phone call. Colin, one the most intense people in the group, was frowning. 'What a wasted opportunity' he said wistfully. 'This is what I usually say:"I'll give you a minute of my time if you give me a minute of yours" and tell them the Good News. The rest of the group looked impressed but Sue felt deflated. She went away from the meeting thinking about how pathetic her attempts at witnessing were. Why couldn't she be more like Colin and spread the message to everyone she came into contact with?

While there are a lot of people who, like Colin, have a knack of communicating the Good News to anyone who crosses their path you will probably be able to identify with Sue. You have never hidden that fact that you are a Christian and you may have even invited your friends and colleagues to special evangelistic events but there are times when you compare yourself to someone like Colin you may feel a bit of a failure.

You may be thinking of ways in which you can be more effective and proactive in your witness. While this is a good thing you should never feel under pressure. Just relax and ask the Lord to help you communicate the good news in the way most suited to your character and gifts. If you are a relational person develop friendships with people and look for opportunities where you can talk about your faith in a natural way. If you have a good grasp of contemporary culture try to discuss the latest films and books from a Christian perspective. For example in the film 'Superman Returns' Superman says to Lois Lane, 'You wrote that the world does not need a saviour, and neither do I. But, every day I hear people crying for one.' You could make the conversation move to the Good News by telling them how it made you think about your relationship with Jesus'. Do not be afraid of attacks on the truth such as 'The Da-Vinci Code', they will give you great openings for conversations and there is a lot of good material available to help you tackle the issues that are raised. It will help the credibility of your arguments if you read the book for yourself.

The most important principle is to be yourself. God uses different people in distinct ways: ask him to show you how he wants to use you.

Chapter Five
Hiccups for youth

IMAGE

'Mum, you can't expect me to wear that!'

Jackie had just been handed a brand new coat; which her mum had carefully and lovingly chosen in the mistaken belief that it was the latest fashion. Two winters ago it would have been seen on just about every teenage girl in the country but it had become yesterday's item destined for the graveyard of fashion. She thought she had uncovered a bargain but had ended up buying her daughter a 'lemon'.

'But I've seen your friends wearing coats like this and you said that you would love to have one.'

Jackie rolled her eyes and waved her hand in the air. 'Mum that was two years ago I wouldn't be seen dead wearing that now.'

From politics to popular culture we live in a society obsessed with image, and school or college can often be the place where your image determines who accepts you and what people think of you. You are probably aware of people who wear certain styles of fashion to identify themselves with a particular group; in effect it becomes a uniform.

Fashion makes a statement. Those who go around dressed in black and embellished with dark make-up will probably take a cynical and rebellious view of life. Women who wear as little as they can, showing as much flesh as possible are saying 'girls just wanna have fun'.

This is a troublesome area for a Christian: you do not want to create unnecessary barriers with other people but neither do you want to be a slave to the latest fashion – especially if it makes a statement that goes against the Bible. Girls are under the most pressure in this area as fashions can involve low-cut or over-tight tops and short skirts that may open them up to temptation and tempt others. Some Christian groups have reacted by telling their women that they should not wear make up or dress in a way that even faintly resembles the latest look. However while the Bible gives clear guidelines on this matter Christians do not have to appear as if they still living in the 1950's. If you put the following principles into practice you will have everything you need to chart a course through the fashion minefield.

- Modesty

'I also want women to dress modestly, with decency and propriety, not with braided hair or gold or pearls or expensive clothes, but with good deeds, appropriate for women who profess to worship God' (1 Timothy 2:9-10).

At the time Paul wrote those words 'braided hair' and 'costly pearls' were associated with prostitutes. He had written the letter to Timothy who was leading a Church in Ephesus. The city was home to the temple of Aphrodite (the Greek goddess of love) which was known for prostitution. These women were recognised by their elaborate hairstyles and ornate jewelry. Some of the Christian women may have been tempted to follow this fashion but Paul forbad it because of its associations and the wrong messages it sent out.

These verses do not prohibit women from having particular hair styles or from wearing jewellery but they do say that Christian women should carefully consider what they wear. Think about the message your clothing sends out. Is it designed to attract the wrong kind of attention or to show as much flesh as possible? Then it is not suitable for someone who wants to follow Christ.

- Authentic Beauty

We are bombarded with adverts marketing products claiming to make people more beautiful. The world sees beauty as something external while the Bible takes a completely contrary position:

> 'Your beauty should not come from outward adornment, such as
> braided hair and the wearing of gold jewellery and fine clothes.
> Instead, it should be that of your inner self, the unfading beauty
> of a gentle and quiet spirit, which is of great worth in God's sight'
> (1 Peter 3:3-4).

This truth will free you from the tyranny of trying to look like others and to attract people through your outward appearance. The beauty this world recognises will fade but there is a beauty you cannot find in fashion magazines or on billboards and it will never diminish.

True freedom

The writer Malcolm Bradbury once wryly said, 'Never despise fashion. It is what we have instead of God.' To many people fashion is a tyrannical power ruling their life and dictating their spending, but Christ has freed from this. Here are some liberating truths that will help you to know this freedom.

#1 God loves you as you are

You never need to change yourself to be accepted by God; he loves you for who you are. In fact he chose you in Christ 'before the creation of the world' (Eph 1:4).

#2 You are accepted by God

Everyone, at some time or another has felt pressured to conform to an image because they want to be accepted. Remember that God has accepted you and has made you righteous before him through his son. Vaughan Roberts said, 'As I grow in understanding of the reality and security of my new identity in Christ I will increasingly be set free from the world's obsession with image. I do not have to keep chasing after the acceptance of others; the Creator of the universe has already accepted me.'[9]

#3 You have been transformed by God

Fashion is never stagnant; it is always looking for new ideas and different ways to express itself. Veteran celebrities such as Madonna and Kylie work hard to re-invent themselves so that they keep one step ahead of fashion. Instead of worrying about changing your outward appearance, concentrate on what God is doing within you. The Bible says: 'If anyone is in Christ he is a new creation. The old has passed away behold the new has come' (2 Cor 5:17).

#4 You have a new mind-set

Before you came to Christ your values and ideas were shaped by the world but they are now shaped by God's Word. You should look at the culture you live in from a very different perspective as you used to. As Paul said to the Christians in Corinth: 'We have stopped evaluating others from a human point of view.

9. Roberts, Vaughan, Battles Christians Face, Authentic Media, London, 2007, Page 14

At one time we thought of Christ merely from a human point of view. How differently we know him now!' (2 Corinthians 5:16 New Living Translation). When you appraise someone by the way they dress and fashions they follow you are conforming to the world's shallow mind-set. Jesus never assessed people by their outward appearance and chose to invest time in those who were left on the fringe of society.

I'M NOT 'IN' WITH THE 'IN CROWD'

If you were ever trying to find Steve, all you needed to do was look for the biggest group of people gathered in the college and he would be in the middle of it. Steve was a strong character who exuded confidence and charisma and had the ability to draw a crowd around him and exert influence on them. In recent years he used this for negative purposes, deriding those who did not share his taste in music and dress sense and ensuring that they were excluded from the group. He had become so confident about his power over the people around him that he started to dare them to do dangerous and illegal acts. Some were told to go and steal from a local shop, others were asked to get illegal drugs to distribute and anyone who refused was treated with scorn and contempt. Recently Mick, one of Steve's closest friends, had become a Christian. He wanted to follow Christ but did not want to cut off ties with his old friends and the key was to make sure that he was no longer under Steve's direct influence or control.

'I have decided to follow Jesus'

You may, like Mick, have been under someone's influence and been anxious to be accepted as part of a group. Now, however, you are a follower of Jesus which requires you to put him first whatever the cost may be. His will must take priority and his Word should be your guide. Once you have established this it will be easier to resist the pressure.

Challenge what is 'cool'

The student had a scornful look on his face, 'You Christians are so boring,' he said, 'you don't know what it is to have fun because you can't get drunk like we do.' Then he sat back on his chair looking smug. However he was not prepared for the answer he got, 'Can you tell me what fun there is in seeing the room spin round, spending half the night with your head down the toilet and then having a terrible headache the next day?' He could not think of anything to say in reply!

Peer pressure arises because people accept that it is fun or 'cool' to get involved in a particular practice. The next time you are made to look like a killjoy because you will not do something that compromises you, challenge the assumption that has been made. Do not make it sound as if you are looking down on anyone but make it clear that you will not accept something just because you are told that it is the 'cool' thing to do. From now on you are going to think for yourself and will be gauging everything by the Bible. You never know what the result will be.

Do not be judgmental

The religious leaders of Jesus' day took great delight in making a public display of their piety and craved the respect of the masses but they looked with disdain on those they considered to be sinners. Jesus opposed their hypocrisy calling them 'blind leaders of the blind' (Matt 15:14 KJV) and drew their hostility because he ate and drank with the dregs of society. People identified a quality in Jesus that they had never seen in these men: he had clear, uncompromising standards yet he was 'a friend of sinners'.

There are times when we as Christians can act like this in the way we seem to consider ourselves better than others and speak of them in a judgmental and derisory way. This kind of attitude will only serve to create more distance. Whilst you must be clear about what the Bible says of their lifestyle and practices you should follow Jesus' example and befriend these people rather than speaking down to them.

Come alongside people

She went to the well in the shimmering mid-day heat. It was the only time she could be sure to get her daily supply of water without overhearing the cruel whispers and enduring nasty looks from the other women. It was not easy being an outcast. This day however, was different: a man was sitting by the well and he asked her for a drink. 'You are a Jew, and I am a Samaritan woman. Why are you asking me for a drink?' she asked. Jesus responded by saying 'If you only knew the gift God has for you and who you are speaking to, you would ask me, and I would give you living water' (John 4.10 New Living Translation).

Jesus did not storm up to the woman at the well and confront her with her immoral lifestyle; instead he came alongside her and found common grounds for a conversation. Neither did Jesus gloss over her sin: he said 'you have had five husbands, and you are not even married to the man you are living with now' (John 4:18 New Living Translation). The result was that she went away telling everyone about 'the Saviour of the world' and others believed in him (see John 4:39-42).

Jesus gave us an invaluable lesson in drawing alongside people. He went to a woman who was an outcast and met her on her own territory. He began the conversation gently yet he did not flinch from telling her some uncomfortable truths. And he told her very clearly and naturally about the new life that she needed.

Your Christian commitment may involve you being shunned by former friends too but that can be a liberating experience freeing you to reach out to those who are not part of any groups. You may feel lonely and rejected but that will help you identify with people on the fringe and open up a whole new mission field to you. Remember that Jesus came 'to seek and to save the lost'.

Chapter Six
Hiccups in Education

THE BIGGEST drawback to school and college is the volume of work that you are given to do. With lessons and lectures during the day and reading and revising at night life can seem as if it is dominated by your education. There are many problems that may emerge during this time and in this chapter we will look at some of the most common.

EXAM FEVER

The date was months away when you began your course but in the busyness of studying it seems to have caught up with you. Normal life is put on hold because you are in the limbo of revision and exams. This can be a very strange time in which you sometimes feel as if you have been removed from the human race! Life revolves around cramming your head with as many facts as possible and sitting one exam after another.

Keep your balance

Hazel worked hard throughout her school years and spent her last few months revising solidly for her exams. Simon, however, took a much more relaxed approach to his education and left revision until the last possible moment. You do not need to guess which of us needed to re-take the exams! The difference between the sexes was cleverly summed up in the book title 'Men are from Mars and Women are from Venus' and is acutely obvious in their respective approaches to study during school years.

We are addressing both sides of the divide in this book and each needs a sense of balance. Generally young men need to get down to studying more seriously whilst girls usually need to go a bit easier on themselves.

If you are one of those people who study solidly make sure you give yourself a break. Your conscience will keep trying to pull your nose back into your books but it needs re-programming before it burns you out. A little leisure time and scheduled breaks will actually make your revision more effective. If you just try to cram in as much as possible you will end up at saturation point. Make sure that you get out in the fresh air and get some exercise, it does not have to be a big work-out at the gym – a brisk walk around the park will work wonders.

Keep your Quiet Times going

Exam season can be so pressurised that it becomes difficult to find time to spend alone with God. In the same way that it is important to have your meals, it is vital to make room in your schedule to be alone with God and to feed on his Word. You may not be able to spare as much time as usual but you could do something a bit different and less demanding until the exams finish. You can find a variety of devotions in Simon's book 'Improving your Quiet Time'. This will be a demanding time and you need the spiritual nurture and strength the Quiet Time will provide.

Have a sense of perspective

Exams can seem like insurmountable challenges when you are in the middle of them but once they are over and your hard work is rewarded with a good grade you will see them in perspective. Try gaining some of that perspective now: it is important to do your best and work hard but the Lord is in control and he does not expect the impossible from you. Write down these verses and look at them every time you feel stressed about your exams or worried about the future. And be certain to read them just before you take each exam:

> 'But I trust in you, O Lord; I say, "You are my God." My times are in your hands' (Psalm 31:14-15)

Ask for God's help

Although it would be wrong to expect the Lord to help you pass an exam when you have been lazy, it is important that while you put the work in, you ask his help to get you through. God is interested in every area of your life – including your studies – and since you are called to 'do everything to the glory of God' (1 Cor 10:31) you should seek to honour him in your revision. Pray about the subjects you struggle with and ask him to help you understand them and to do well. This will be a great witness to your friends. Exams are seen as the doorway to success and advancement: something upon which your future depends. As a Christian your approach should have a different emphasis: 'you are working for the Lord not for men' (Col 3:23) and you can safely leave your future in his hands.

Plan carefully

When Simon was taking some important exams he received some great help from a friend who had been disciplined and successful in his studies. He recommended that Simon listed the subjects in order of difficulty and apportioned time for each one, giving a little extra to the more difficult ones. If an exam for a particular subject was at a later date, more time could be given after the others were finished.

Don't neglect worship

Hebrews tells us 'not to give up the habit of meeting together' (Heb 10:25) and it gives no exception for exam time! Your determination to do well may make you want to stay at home and revise on a Sunday rather than gather with God's people but God's Word cuts right across that idea. You need the support and encouragement of your fellowship and youth group more than ever during this time. Try to follow the principle of setting Sunday aside to rest. One wise father used to encourage his daughter to do so saying: 'it is common sense as well as God's law to set aside a day to rest.'

Be nice to your family

We worked it right: there are three years between our sons which meant that they were not taking exams at the same time! A home that is dominated by exams can be a very tense place and you may not realize that you might be the cause of it. Revision will be much less stressful if you show kindness and love to your family.

AM I ON THE WRONG COURSE?

It looked so interesting and promising when she first applied for the course but a term into it Alex was wondering whether she had made the right choice. Despite taking advice from her teachers and praying about whether to take the course she was interested in, she now had a horrible feeling that she had made a mistake and she did not know what to do next.

Knock out the nonsense

If you find yourself in the same position, you must not think that you have made such a big mistake that you will never recover from it. We knew someone who was tortured by these thoughts during his first year at Theological College. He used to tell us that he thought he would never be able to get into ministry because he had not attended the right college: he has been a Pastor since he graduated! Even if you have not made the right decision, God is in control and he will 'work all things together for the good of those who love him' (Rom 8:28). Do not let Satan pull you down with thoughts that you have blown your chances – that is complete nonsense.

Talk to someone

Instead of keeping this to yourself talk to someone who will be able to help you such as a tutor or career advisor. Write down your difficulties before you speak to them so that you ensure that everything is covered. Listen carefully to their advice and then give yourself some time to think and pray about it.

Take action

If, after getting advice, you are still unhappy about your course you are free to change. It may cause some inconvenience to you and your family and you may even to wait until the next academic year. But you should not feel obliged to carry on studying a subject you cannot get on with.

Take your time before committing to a new subject

Rather than rush into committing yourself to a different course get some temporary work so that you can think carefully about what you should do next. Ask yourself what your long-term goals are and what you enjoy doing. Contrary to many people's understanding God does not want you to go into a career that you do not like and cannot do very well in – he wants you to enjoy your work.

Education is a great privilege providing many opportunities to tell others about the Good News. It is also full of challenges and temptations that you will need to overcome. We hope that this chapter has helped you to do so.